THE SPOOKY TALES

A BOOK OF HORROR FOLKLORE

KARAN MOHAN THAKUR

Contents

By the pricking of my thumbs,
Something wicked this way comes.
(Macbeth, WILLIAM SHAKESPEARE)

CHAPTER ONE

THE SEVEN RULERS OF HELL

The seven rulers of damnation is a thought; we referenced that when we examined Lucifer, but it's not referenced unequivocally in the sacred text. However, it is an intriguing thought that numerous researchers have endeavored to clarify over the most recent 600 years.We will investigate a portion of these thoughts, generally zeroing in on the characterization of devils by Diminish Binsfeld, which acquires vigorously from the possibility of the seven savage sins.

Subside Binsfeld was a German diocesan and strict researcher, conceived in Germany in 1540 or 1545, contingent upon fluctuating sources. As a kid, Dwindle was skilled enough to be shipped off to Rome to consider. At the point when he returned, he turned into an exact figure in numerous enemy Protestant missions. What he was most notable for was the part he played in the witch preliminaries of Trier that occurred from 1581 until 1593. Binsfeld composed a compelling piece named The Admissions of Warlocks and Witches, which contained the supposed admissions of these people that had been acquired through torment and consequently, as indicated by him, ought to be accepted and trusted.

This is significant because, at the time, Diminish was viewed as a somewhat clever man, a specialist in religion and its heavenly components. In 1589, among the confusion of these witch preliminaries, he distributed top-notch evil spirits that he accepted to be the rulers or rulers of damnation.

As indicated by Binsfeld, the seven destructive sins, or more than simply fatal indecencies. He accepted everyone was, actually, an evil spirit. So who are these evil spirits?

The first of these is **Lucifer**, who spoke to the transgression of pride, the first and generally genuine of the seven destructive sins. In such a manner, Binsfeld is alluding to Lucifer, the fallen blessed messenger. His mind-boggling pride prompted him to accept that he could manage paradise. Thus he was projected out and vilified when his defiance was fruitless. They present a token of the threats when one permits pride to beat them. Some believe Lucifer to be the leader of the seven rulers. These records regularly trust Lucifer and Satan are similar people. Different arrangements who disagree consider Satan the nonentity of heck, a substance separate from Lucifer. Even now and then, they supplant Lucifer with another fallen heavenly attendant figure, for example, Azazel.

The second devil Binsfeld refers to is **Mammon**, whose name generally means mean cash, and I'm sure you've speculated he is the exemplification of our next transgression, covetousness. In the sacred text, Mammon isn't a physical being, all the more so an idea encompassing cash, abundance, and desire. Over the long run, this started to change. What's more, it was during Medieval times. Mammon turned out to be something other than an idea. He was exemplified as the evil presence of insatiability in various bits of craftsmanship and writing. In this manner, a few researchers started to group him as one of the sovereigns of damnation who might oppress the individuals driven by avarice and the aggregation of abundance now and again and can be mistaken for Satan. What's more, however, the two of them can be viewed as devils of eagerness, gluttony, and greed aren't something very similar.

The third Ruler of damnation is **Asmodeus**, who spoke to the wrongdoing of desire; the more significant part of what we think about Asmodeus originates from the Book of Tobit, just as some other Talmudic stories, for example, the development of the Sanctuary of Solomon. Many considered his to be spreading desire through the land from average citizens to lords and sovereigns. No one was sheltered. In the book of Tobit, he went gaga for a lady named Sarah and kept her from wedding to any other person. He also slaughtered seven of her better half the evening of their wedding, not long before they could perfect the marriage. The eighth spouse, Tobias, was fortunate enough not to endure a comparative destiny; following exhortation given to him by the Archangel Raphael, he had the option to repulse the evil spirit. He set a fish's heart and liver over some consuming coals, and when Asmodeus visited them that night, the smell made him escape, where Raphael would later limit him. In the Commentary and the confirmation of Solomon, Asmodeus has various experiences with Solomon. An entry references his wedding to Lillith and accepts her as his evil presence sovereign. His appearance can differ; however, more often than not, we see a section man, part creature crossbreed. The Cabala clarifies this as him being a Cambian, a half-human, half-evil presence posterity, his mom a succubus, and his dad, Lord David.

The fourth devil ruler, as per Binsfeld, was **Leviathan**, which spoke to the wrongdoing of jealousy. This one may appear somewhat odd, as when many people think about the Leviathan, they think about a gigantic ocean beast, not something you'd expect would be found in damnation. It has many understandings and implications for various religions. However, this relationship with envy and the sovereigns of damnation that Binsfeld discusses is a Christian idea. The Italian thinker and Catholic cleric Thomas Aquinas depicted it as a devil answerable for rebuffing those blameworthy of jealousy by gulping down them. Leviathan was additionally regularly observed as speaking to the doors of hellfire. In Somewhat English Saxon artistry, the passage to damnation was viewed as the vast mouth of a beast known as the Hellmouth, or the jaws of heck, with a leviathan viewed as a wide range of animals from a goliath ocean snake to an enormous whale or even a crocodile. The animals expanding more was probably sufficient to impact this Old English Saxon theme.

The fifth devil ruler is **Beelzebub**, the master of gluttony; another name you may observe is the Master of Flies or the Ruler of Flyes, which alludes to his ability to fly. Lucifer is a figure who can be followed back through various human advancements and religions. In the confirmation of Solomon, he is a fallen holy messenger, frequently connected with Lucifer. He doesn't have a specific space. He acts nonexclusive and evil, making men love devils and turn on one another, capitulating to desire, envy, and murder. Simply an overall instigator. The Dutch demonologist Johann Vier considered him the central lieutenant to Lucifer and fundamental to a fruitful rebel against the fiend. John Milton likewise shared this view in Heaven Lost. Lucifer is a fallen heavenly attendant who, alongside Asteroth, is second just to Lucifer regarding the chain of importance. Binsfeld thinks of him as the Ruler of intemperance is challenging to state, as others compared him to bogus divine beings, pride and jealousy.

The sixth evil spirit sovereign is without a doubt the most notable **Satan**, the Master of Rage; as this is Diminish Binsfeld's grouping, we can accept when he says Satan, he's alluding to the Christian understanding in the early current time frame from around the sixteenth century onwards, soon after the Medieval times, from around 1480 onwards, the delirium around witches started to twisting crazy. France and Binsfeld's local Germany were two of the most famous models in some European nations.

Heinrich Kramer and Jacob Springers, "Malleus Maleficarum," were distributed in 1487, which clarifies that Satan crafted all witchcraft. Furthermore, we see Satan's relationship with warlocks and witches in Medieval times. Satan was constantly portrayed as sad and horrendous, with no genuine force. In any case, presently, with a dread of black magic on the ascent, satan would usually turn into a devil that individuals dreaded, to such an extent that the congregation dismissed its consideration from other religions. The center was currently around Satan.

Their straightforward confidence in him was thought to lead Christians adrift.

Our last evil spirit ruler is **Belphegor**. The Master of Sloth. Binsfeld considered him to be the head of lethargy. Also, however, he has a point; there is a whole other world to his character. You wouldn't be right to contend that he is more qualified as the Ruler of control and trickery. Belphegor takes numerous structures, picking whichever one he feels will persuade his casualties into making his offering. He convinces, entices, and controls people into making promising innovations that will make them rich, a murmur, or a push in a specific way that prompts astonishing revelations. However, when these are finished, the riches and regard are grabbed away by Belphegor. He may not be the most forcing and all the more alarming devil; however, Belphegor is probably remarkably tricky and beguiling.

Various arrangements of devils exist by a wide range of researchers, and we've barely taken a gander at one. If you'd prefer to do some further perusing and perceive how they contrast, you can pursue the order of devils and discover a large group of fluctuating thoughts you can analyze.

CHAPTER TWO

Lucifer: The Fallen Angel

The name Lucifer invokes various pictures, and the most widely recognized is that of Satan or the demon, a holy messenger who transgressed and defied God, a figure who exists to entice a man and lady into wrongdoing. This widespread thought can be found in various religions and convictions. In any case, as far as demonology, Lucifer speaks to one of the seven lethal sins, the wrongdoing of pride.

The Book of Disclosures depicts a war that occurred in paradise between the holy messengers; the individuals who lost would be projected from heaven and left to possess the earth. At that point, war broke out in paradise. Michael and his holy messengers battled against the mythical serpent and the monster, and his heavenly attendants retaliated. In any case, he was insufficient, and they lost their place in paradise. The incredible monster was holding down that old snake called the villain or Satan, who drives the world adrift.

He was flung practical and his heavenly attendants with him. This story has been deciphered in a few different ways. Some accept this monster alludes to Lucifer, the most delightful of God's heavenly attendants. However, with this came a massive measure of pride, and Lucifer, before long, started to scrutinize his maker and everything around him. He viewed himself as not the same as different blessed messengers. He would not acknowledge the universe in its present status, and as his distrustfulness developed, he trusted God himself was imperfect and that he was the main wonderful being left.

In his sunrise of God, he was in good company as he figured out how to persuade 33% of the holy messengers in paradise to join his motivation. The primary activity against God was aimed at his valued creation of 'humanity .'God's enthusiasm for people is something that Lucifer would never comprehend. They were very defective creatures, and he could never bow down to such a mediocre creation.

He persuaded the Archangel Samael to appear as a snake and entice Eve into taking the taboo organic product, making both Adam and Eve be projected from the Nursery of Eden. He, at that point, persuaded 33% of the holy messengers in paradise to favor him in this disobedience to God. Also, when the ideal opportunity for war came, he changed himself into a great winged serpent. On one side stood Lucifer and the blessed messengers who needed change. On the opposite side stood a more considerable armed force driven by the Archangel Michael. What's more, this war would seethe on for a long time. Yet, in the long run, Michael, when the holy messengers who favored him and God would raise victors and Lucifer, this extraordinary mythical beast, was projected from paradise, and every one of the individuals who lined up with him would experience the ill effects of elegance.

There was additionally a recounting of this story where Lucifer is projected from paradise and looks for vengeance against God with the making of Adam and Eve; Lucifer was not, at this point, God's most loved being. So what is preferable retribution over the heresy of humanity? When they were made, Adam and Eve were told by God never to eat from the information tree. Lucifer would mask himself as a snake and lure Eve into taking a nibble of the prohibited natural product. Accordingly, they would likewise be projected from the Nursery of Eden.

The story itself can be very befuddling because some accept the snake may have been the Archangel Samael making the offering of

Satan. Others contend the snake was, in reality, Lucifer, in addition to the fact that he takes the type of a monster, but at the same time, he's alluded to like that old snake. It's never clarified in any detail. So it just boils down to how you decipher the sacred writings and stories. A few references make it simple to draw this association between Satan and Lucifer.

In Isaiah 14, 12 through 15. It says, "How all of you tumbled from paradise—o day Star, Child of First light, how you are chopped to the cold earth. You who laid the country's low said in your heart, and I will climb to paradise over the stars of God. I will set my seat on high. I will sit on the Mount of Get together in the most distant ranges of the north. I will climb over the statures of mists. I will make myself like the highest. Yet, you are brought down to shield the pit's furthest reaches".

In Hebrew, the prophet Isaiah denounces the ruler of Babylon in a dream and is called Halil Ben-Shahar, which implies the child of the morning or sparkling one. This was then deciphered by the Greeks and Romans to mean Morningstar or Light Bearer, and this lord would then become Lucifer. Along these lines, this entry in Isaiah can be viewed as itemizing the fall of Lucifer from paradise, how he planned to put himself above God and take the seat for himself, yet instead wound up in hellfire.

Ezekiel, 28 17 additionally specifies this transgress. "Your heart was glad because of your excellence. You adulterated your insight for your quality. I cast you to the ground. I uncovered you before rulers to confront their eyes on you". These entries show Lucifer as the fallen blessed messenger. It isn't until the record of the battle in paradise. In the Book of Disclosures, we referenced prior that this fall has a place with Satan.

What's more, he told them; I saw Satan fall like lightning from paradise. No notice of the morning star or a fallen heavenly attendant. It's Satan or, in disclosure, a winged serpent. With this change comes an adjustment in appearance. Lucifer, the morning star, the most delightful of God's manifestations, would have been a brilliant being.

Be that as it may, with this transgress and demonization, Lucifer would look more sinister. His once excellent feathered wings would be more webbed like a bat's. His face was distorted and contorted, and on his head sat horns. What was previously a wondrous thing at that point turned into a thing of fear, with pictures of Satan not, in any event, looking like a human structure. All the more so a devilish goat man with wings. The relationship with the cunning warlocks and witches came with this change into Satan. Subside Binsfield recognized seven evil presences delegated to the sovereigns of heck, each related to one of the seven fatal sins. Lucifer spoke to the wrongdoing of pride.

Dante's Inferno likewise has an intriguing inter- predation of Satan, which I won't broadly expound. Dante's Satan is a vast evil presence with bat-like wings, and three faces solidified in the ice at the focal point of hellfire. He likewise realizes that Satan was previously a heavenly attendant of light known as Lucifer. Where Dante contrasts with different creators is standing out; he depicts Satan as peculiar, still, and incapable of talking like a goliath drooling mass. He isn't the leader of damnation. He leaves as a detainee and gets similar discipline as every other delinquent, which is different from the Lucifer we find in the next bit of writing.

The Book of Disclosures doesn't say straightforwardly that Lucifer and Satan are similar substances. However, this association between Lucifer and Satan is one that creators and history specialists have adorned and created throughout the long term. One of the most renowned instances of this would be John Milton's epic sonnet Heaven Lost. This story follows the fall of humanity and one specific blessed messenger. Milton's Satan was Lucifer, one of the paradise's most excellent blessed messengers. He wouldn't reply to the desire of God since holy messengers are brought up themselves. They had no mother and no dad. So for what reason should God have authority over them? It's wiser to reign in hellfire than serve in paradise. Milton's character is both sly and appealing. Even though Lucifer and his adherents lost this war and were projected from heaven, he was as yet ready to get the force he wanted as he would reign in damnation with the individuals who favored him. Milton, as it were, he gallantly paints Lucifer. What's more, you could contend this is because he spoke to Milton's convictions.

He wasn't the greatest fan of the Lord of Britain and accepted he ought to be toppled as he felt a parliament would be considerably more delegate of the individuals. Lucifer isn't excessively quite the same as Milton taking that the heavenly attendants ought to oversee themselves. Rather than explaining God. In Heaven Lost, Milton outlines God as an authoritative pioneer, and those restricted to him endure his anger. Not very unique to how he saw the Ruler of Britain. Lucifer, for instance, lost to everything. From the start, he lost his magnificence and status in paradise, and he was not God's number one creation at this point. But then we observe this thought that it's wiser to administer in hellfire than to live in paradise under oppression. The battle in heaven was lost. However, Lucifer accomplished his objective.

Even though it's exceptionally regular to take a gander at Satan as pure fiendishness, Lucifer, then again, gives us a significantly more relatable and fascinating character. We see that today, regularly in present-day fiction, he's in no way, shape, or form a signal of light or even a saint. In any case, there is a particular interest in his story. On the off chance that we pad down the fall of Lucifer, its majority originates from interest, needing to scrutinize the condition of the universe and not just acknowledge the standards that have been spread out before him by another person. On the off chance that you follow the scriptural sacred texts, at that point, Lucifer's pride is the transgression that prompts fiendishness and his ruin.

In any case, on the off chance that you approach the story in a less scriptural style, as Milton does in Heaven Lost, it's Lucifer posing a progression of inquiries about the world he lives in and concluding he would not like to be administered by another person he doesn't accept speaks to him or different holy messengers. You could contend that this is because the thought processes behind these accounts are not equivalent. The scriptural stories are a warning for the individuals who wish to challenge the expression of God for their benefit, decrying the individuals who do. Milton's work, then again, is an encouragement to challenge overbearing guidelines or the norm on the off chance it doesn't speak to you or the individuals around you.

Lucifer is undoubtedly a fascinating figure. Regardless of whether you sense that you can comprehend the thinking behind his activities or accept that he is the fiend of works like Heaven Lost and even the later Lucifer Television program, at any rate, posed the inquiry. Would he say he is that evil? The appropriate response lies with you.

CHAPTER THREE

Lilith: Mother of Demons

When taking a gander at demonology and the different figures that show up all through religion, there is one female figure; one name more so than some other, that has risen above various societies and even right up ‘til today still regularly shows up as a character in a wide range of mainstream society.

Furthermore, that name is Lilith. The most well-known portrayal of Lilith, in any case, is as an evil spirit of the night, enchanting and sexual, yet additionally savage. What's more, if that wasn't sufficient, she likewise holds up until the front of dimness to take infants and small kids. This idea can be followed right back to antiquated Mesopotamian religion, where there once existed a figure known as Lamashtu, the girl of the sky God Ano. To a few, she was a disgusting goddess. To other people, an evil spirit, a beast that plagues ladies during labor, one that would take their kids, suck out their blood and marrow, know on the bones that remain.

The moms are undependable of Lamashtu, and neither will their unborn youngsters, as she could cause ladies to prematurely deliver as one of the most startling devils in Mesopotamian fantasy. Her activities were not simply restricted to pregnant ladies. She would drink the blood and eat the substance of men. She tainted one's fantasies until just bad dreams were left. She was trailed by infection, illness, and demise anywhere she went. Of these accounts of Lamashtu, we can see a correspondence with animals, for example, vampires and succubi.

Today many consider Lilith the primary spouse of Adam, who revolted and was later supplanted by Eve. This thought originates from the Book of Beginning, the whole first book in both the Jewish Book of scriptures and the Old Confirmation. It was beginning one subtleties the making of the universe just as everything within it. It says that God made the sky, the earth, vegetation, creatures, and in conclusion, humankind in his picture to lead over what he had made.

What's imperative to note is that beginning, one expresses that he made both man and lady simultaneously. Beginning two is fundamentally the same as talking about the production of the universe. However, it varies concerning the formation of man and lady.

Here, the man was made first, not needing his creation to be distant from everyone else. God sent the man into a profound sleep and took from him a rib which he would use to make the prominent lady. So basically, you have two negating records of our creation, one after the other.

To many, the expression of God is consecrated and, like this, can't repudiate itself. This prompted researchers to clarify the contrasts between Beginning one and two as portraying two separate functions instead of two records of a similar position. This, in turn, made the requirement for a story that clarifies these distinctions, which would be found in what is alluded to as midrash.

The clarification here is that God expected to make a lady twice, once with the man and afterward with the man. The lady in the main story isn't recognized initially; however, she is known as Lilith in the long run. The lady in the following story is who we know from the Holy book as Eve.

So if you've ever heard the account of Eve being made from Adam's rib, that is the story found in Beginning two. Lilith also shows up in the Commentary, and these records are far less vague than we see in the beginning. She shows up here an aggregate of multiple times and is never alluded to as Adam's significant other, whereas the Babylonians alluded to Lilu as winged male evil spirits. The Writing discusses Lilith or Lilitu as an evil presence with wings and the essence of a lady.

It says that Lilith might seize a man dozing in a house alone. It said that she gathered the semen of men while they stayed in bed to make more devil posterity, which again can be viewed as perhaps the most punctual case of the succubus.

She is likewise connected with a few evil presences, one of which is the Agarath, a night devil who goes after kids and the powerless.

Until this point, we can see two particular pictures of Lilith, the lady and the evil spirit. In any case, what occurred in this center ground from when she was made as far as possible until she turned into a devil?

Stories disclosing this will create considerably more detail about the Medieval times. So from the fifth century to the fifteenth, subtleties of Ben Sira and the letters in order of Serac are bits of work that reverberate an opinion that numerous researchers and copyists appear to concur upon.

At the point when Adam and Lilith were made, neither one of them needed to submit to the next. This implied who accepted the prevailing party in the relationship to a few. In contrast, others interpreted this as meaning neither one needed to expect the base situation during sex as it was an indication of compliance, with neither one ready to settle.

Lilith, at that point, fled the Nursery of Eden. For all to hear, she articulated God's real name, and in doing so, she turned into a wing evil spirit in a flash. At the point when the blessed messengers sought after her with expectations of bringing her back. She disclosed to them she had no aim of returning. As discipline for her defiance, the three holy messengers who discovered her guarantee to kill 100 of her evil presence kids each day. Her motivation presently was unique to make disease and ailment the babies of others.

At whatever point a youngster was conceived, she would guarantee domain over that kid for eight days if they were a kid and 20 on the off chance they were a young lady. With this, they came just one trade-off. At whatever point she saw the name of any of these three holy messengers engraved on an emblem or a talisman, that youngster would be disregarded. There isn't a lot of enduring material from the Akkadian domain that considers an inside and out examination of Lamashtu or the Lilitu corresponding to Lilitu.

However, we know from the Babylonians and Sumerians that these animals were comparable. What's more, it is anything but a vast stretch to state that they may have impacted Lilith's story here and there. The absence of data concerning her source is compensated for by how mainstream her story was.

The Medieval times denoted this period like no other, with various indicators and translations. Portrayals of her changed from a lovely lady to a more evil devil. Moreover, some even considered her the snake in the Nursery of Eden, enticing Eve with the prohibited natural product as one last demonstration of retribution. As time passed, some people's stories considered Lilith a devil sovereign and accordingly identified with Asmodeus, who many consider the lord of evil presences. Asmodeus has been referenced in the Book of Tobit; the Writing and various sacred texts imply it's not generally an immense shock that he and Lilith showed up together as the mother and father of devils.

Together, they had many devil kids and headed out from town to town, causing disarray and obliteration. In certain accounts, she's also firmly connected with Samael, a somewhat odd character. A few lessons in the Secrecy go as far as to state that Lilith was Samuel's associate and that it was not God who made her, but rather Samael, who made himself an evil spirit spouse who filled the job later expected for Eve.

He additionally gave her a large group of evil kids, one of these being Asmodeus, who we referenced prior. All through these accounts, there are three fundamental signs, the Lillith, the one who defied God and Adam, the side we see the least of, the alluring evil spirits which plague the fantasies of men to develop her satanic family, and in conclusion. This beast went after pregnant ladies eating up their kids.

At the point when I previously read about Lilith, I quickly drew a few equals between her and a portion of the animals we find in Greek folklore. At the point when you think about a terrible and harmful fowl like an animal, the shrews unquestionably ring a bell. Be that as it may, so do the alarms have a more beautiful nature.

Notwithstanding, the character who nearest looks like and typifies these three indications of Lilith is Lamia. These three phases are nearly reflected in her story, she starts as a customary lady who succumbs to desire, and accordingly, her youngsters are slaughtered as a discipline.

She's at that point changed into a beast in some telling Lamia and the Lamai of vampiric devils who feed off the blood of youthful, attractive men. There are likewise forms of this story where rather than youngsters, she chases for kids perpetually, looking for retribution for those she had lost. Much like Lilith, Lamia was expected to be a wake-up call, a boogeyman-like figure. However, her story is substantially less about insubordination and more about the threats of desire.

Indeed, accounts of Lilith are somewhat befuddling; it's just truly due to stories from midrash and different researchers that we can even draw a connection between the evil spirit and the spouse of Adam. Notwithstanding, this hasn't generally hurt her portrayal in mainstream society.

There are a couple of references that I recall, yet investigating it further, I was undoubtedly astounded that various books, films, games, and Programs that her name shows up and fans of Narratives of Narnia could realize that the White, which is a relative of the primary spouse of Adam, which for this situation is, Lillith in the Network program Genuine Blood and the film 30 Days of Night, Lilith shows up as the name of a vampire.

Furthermore, this is a significant basic pattern when she shows up;

it's either as a succubus or a vampire.
Old-school extraordinary fans may recollect her as the principal human to be enticed by Lucifer into turning into a devil.
Talking about Lucifer in that show, she's additionally alluded to as the mother of evil spirits, one that I miss that has a strict fascinating interpretation of Lilith's story is the fifth component, which sounds very odd to state, thinking of it as modern science fiction.
Lilith was depicted along these lines as Adam's first spouse and her talking antiquated Aramaic bodes well than when I viewed the film as a child; rather than crushing humanity, she winds up sparing it, turning the first story on its head. With regards to video games, on the off chance that you've played anything distantly mainstream, it's probably because you've seen her name someplace, as it shows up in Conclusive Dream, Borderlands, Diablo, Darksiders, Devil May Cry, and many, some more. I think Lilith has an intriguing story, paying little heed to how befuddling and line together the first references might be, regardless of whether you consider it to be a transgressor or a defiant uprising; it's a general idea, which is the reason I believe it's referred to so regularly today.

It might likewise have something to do with the mysterious and current dream going inseparably.

CHAPTER FOUR

CODEX GIGAS: THE DEVIL'S BIBLE

In the Thirteenth century, inside a Benedictine religious community in archaic Bohemia, a priest named Hermann perpetrated a horrendous outrage, breaking his devout promises and justified capital punishment. He was bricked behind the thick dividers of the abbey, disregarded to starve.

Before the last block was put, Hermann called out for kindness to go along with him. The abbot struck an outlandish arrangement. He was to make a book of all the world's information joined and do it in a solitary night. Urgently, Herman acknowledged the materials were pushed into the little hole in the divider. The priest burned through no time in the beginning; however, as the night went on, reality set in the errand was unthinkable, and Herman was destined to bomb except if.

There was one final thing he could deal with, his spirit. That night, the priest traded his Soul to the demon for a finished book, a fantastic book of the world's most prominent functions, as a gesture of appreciation. The priest drew a full-page picture of the field. The following morning, Hermann gave the Book to the abbot, saving his life.

This legend has been told since not long after the Book's creation and has some legitimacy.

There are certain angles about the Book that, right up until the present time, leave archeologists and history specialists confounded and uncertain how the Book, known as the Codex Gigas or the Devil's Book of scriptures, was even composed.

On the head of this are legends of a revile that has followed the fiend's Book of scriptures consistently.

The Codex Gigas, Latin for the monster book, is known by that name for one explanation, its fantastic size, 36 inches tall, 20 inches wide, and almost nine inches thick; this tremendous work weighs as much personally.

At 165 pounds, it requires two custodians to lift; its coupling is produced using cowhide and fancy metal as pages are made out of the skins of, in any event, 160 jackasses.

Inside the Book, each page is formed fastidiously and with an ability no lesser than outright authority, down to the enlightenment of each letter as portrayed inside the legend. The world's information inside incorporates the Latin Book of scriptures, just as Isidore of civils, reference book historical background, Josephson's Ancient pieces of the Jews, and Cosmas of Progs Narrative of Bohemia. Numerous more modest writings are scattered through prominent compositions on wizardry recipes, expulsion customs, and a schedule. Similarly, as with any nice secret of history, ten pages are inquisitively absent.

Nobody is sure what they contained or why they were eliminated.

Those pages have never been recuperated, other than his physical size, its most celebrated component is an unusual full-page portrayal of the devil on page 290.

This massive animal fills the generally empty page in a whole tone and one-of-a-kind detail with his threatening gaze, bent hooks, red horns, and two tongues. He is bare except for an ermine undergarment. History specialists note that Ermin is worn by sovereignty. In this portrayal, the fallen angel wears ermine to connote himself as the Sovereign of murkiness.

The unusual unevenness between the composition's determined scrupulousness and its sheer extension obscures the lines between fantasy and the truth. Stop and think for a minute. The content is intensely enlightening. I don't get this' meaning. Pages and letters are enhanced with unbelievable expertise, all through slight delineations, expound fringes, adapted, and enlivened letters. Unbelievably, and a few specialists state inconceivably, the idea of composing is uniform. There are no recognizable indications of progress in look or quality, not even in the smallest.

We can make two determinations from this. To start with, the Codex Gigas was composed of a solitary recorder.

Second, the puzzling consistency from start to finish recommends that it might have been written in an exceptionally brief timeframe. Here falsehoods are the issue. The composition specialists state this is absurd. The monstrous degree of detail and vast assortments of writings would have assumed control over five years of endless composing throughout the day and the entire night to finish. All things being equal, this gauge avoids numerous outlines.

The Master expresses that it would have taken, in any event, 25 years to compose an almost certain 30. Notwithstanding, there is, as yet, the issue of consistency.

Why does the copyist not indicate maturing, ailment, temperament, or expanded expertise? How might somebody compose for a very long time without faltering in nature or quality?

These unsolved inquiries give the legend of the Devil's Book of scriptures a run for its cash. Specialists don't know how such fastidious consistency is feasible for such a timeframe.

Indeed, even with great expectation and devotion, physical constraints to the human body accompany age, such as vision crumbling or joint inflammation.

Then again, we should investigate the picture of the demon as history is one of the Book's essential central focuses throughout the codex. The Book was shown with this page open.

Yet, numerous individuals don't know that there is another complete page delineation legitimately close to it that we can't state without a doubt. Specialists accept that this portrays the realm of paradise. So as the Book is shown open, this twofold page spread represents the duality between great and wickedness.

For this situation, maybe the drawing of the fallen angel is a warning from the second instead of a tribute of appreciation.

More inquiries emerge when investigating the copyists' signatures found inside the content. It peruses Hermanus and Crucis. This little detail could uphold or sabotage the Fallen angel's Book of scriptures legend. Hermanus is, obviously, the priest's name, Hermann. What's more, the nearest, however, can be deciphered.

Both two different ways in Latin comprehensive could connote a sickening discipline following the first fantasy, be that as it may, it could likewise be deciphered as willful segregation, subsequently the closeness to the English word loner. In this view, the recorder might have decided to withdraw from society and commit himself to his all-consuming purpose. So there are unquestionably contentions for and against the legend puzzling birthplaces aside, there is one more legend that continues with this Book, The Scourge of the Fiend's Book of scriptures.

The Codex Gigas has experienced damnation and its proprietors with it during that time.

Regardless of whether it's actual, we should go along with this for a moment. In 1477, 200 or so years after his creation, the Benedictine religious community in Bohemia encountered some real money-related burdens. To take care of the tabs, the priests chose to sell their generally valuable and disguised fortune quite a while ago—the codex gigas to the Benedictine abbey in Brevinof. Not long after the first abbey was demolished during the upheaval, the Book was kept and severed until 1593, when they loaned the Codex Gigas to Blessed Roman Ruler Rudolph, the second in Prague.

Obviously, to their karma, he chose to stay away forever from the Book. History specialists have uncovered that when Rudolph pre-involved the codex, he focused on the mysterious.

As years passed, his standard became progressively distrustful and flighty. His family paid heed to his fanatical conduct and ousted his situation as Lord. Rudolf kicked the bucket in 1612, yet the codex remained. After six years, the thirty years' war started. This fierce war finished with the Swedish armed forces holding onto the late Rudolf's whole assortment of books and craftsmanship and finding its unmissable fortune, Codex Gigas. It was brought to its last home, the Imperial Library, in Stockholm; however, the revile was not yet wrapped up. In 1697, a wildfire overwhelmed the Illustrious Château in a final desperate attempt to spare the Book. It was tossed out of a close-by window, falling on and harming a clueless onlooker. Even though a significant part of the alleged revile can be credited to the simple occurrence, practically tame contrasted with different condemnations, this frightful notoriety of the Fallen angel's Book of scriptures is undoubtedly not a cutting-edge development.

Consistently, individuals have felt and dreaded its foreboding atmosphere. However, this stroll through history raises one final purpose of interest. If this was, or is to be sure, a malicious book, we need to confront how it endured the Probe in some way or another. During the examination, the Catholic Church had almost complete standards over Europe, and anything regarded sinister or even distantly against the eventual benefits of the congregation was methodically searched out and wrecked or tormented and executed on account of individuals. This time, much information and authentic records were lost, yet not the Codex Gigas. It is a standout amongst other saved middle age original copies we have today. However, countless inquiries stay like those ten pages, torn and lost. Also, what of the confounding riddle of the unwavering handwriting of the recorder? As it's been said, the unseen details are the main problem in every letter.

CHAPTER FIVE

THE SALEM WITCH TRIALS

In the last part of the 1600s, a progression of allegations brought about almost two dozen individuals in New Britain being executed for probably rehearsing black magic. This occurrence has gotten known as the Salem witch preliminaries. Who were the blamed witches? What made this happen? In sixteen hundred's provincial America, faith in the extraordinary was highly ordinary. Numerous individuals credited bombing crops, family diseases, or passing to black magic. For instance, if the family's animals had startlingly kicked the bucket, this may have been viewed as a sign that a witch had to revile their family.

These convictions helped fuel the madness in Salem, Massachusetts, in 1692. In late January and early February in 1692, two young ladies living in Salem Town, Betty Paris, age nine, and Abigail Williams, age 11, started showing abnormal conduct. The young ladies tossed things, shouted, wedged themselves underneath furniture, made peculiar sounds, and contorted into unnatural positions. They likewise grumbled about odd sensations, for example, the inclination that they were being pricked with pins.

Different young ladies inside the town likewise started showing comparative indications. However, the specialist who analyzed every one of them could locate no realized physical sickness tormenting them. Certain people inside the network became persuaded that the young ladies had been reviled by black magic.

Different endeavors were made to recognize who the witch may be. For instance, a touch test was utilized. While one of the casualties was having a fit, a gathering of blamed ladies was asked to lay their hands on her each. On the off chance that the fit died, whoever was contacting her at that point was blamed for being the witch who had reviled her. Another strategy used to recognize the witch was known as a witch cake. A cake was made utilizing Raimele and pee from the affected young lady. The cake was then said to a canine. The conviction was that the witch would encounter exceptional physical torment when the cake was eaten, which would recognize her as a witch. Sarah Great. Sarah Osborne and a slave lady named Tituba were the initial three to be captured.

Sarah Great was a vagrant who had likely been blamed just because of her notoriety in the network. Sarah Osborne seldom went to chapel, and the residents accepted she just had her circumstance as a primary concern. For quite some time, Tituba had engaged the neighborhood young ladies with tales about witches and fortune-telling games. The residents of Salem Town and close by Salem town started seeing black magic all over the place. In the Spring of 1692, four additional ladies were captured. One was captured basically because she set out to address whether the young lady's side effects were genuine or if they were imagined. Another was charged because she wore dark apparel and different outfits, which the townspeople esteemed odd.

In 1692, more allegations were made, more people were captured in the homes of the blamed, ladies were looked at, and any proof was taken advantage of as black magic. On the off chance that enslaved people or mending spices were discovered, this was proof that they may be witches. Many of these ladies had such things since they went about as birthing assistants, nurtured, or helped locals who were wiped out. The blamed individuals were set to be investigated if they were seen as liable; the discipline was demise.

When the insanity finished, 19 individuals had been hanged, 14 ladies and five men, and one man was squashed underneath a heap of substantial stones. Nobody is sure what caused the unexpected frenzy over witches in Salem Town and close by Salem town in 1692. Some have essentially credited the madness to mass psychogenic ailment or widespread panic. Wild allegations and dread filled the craze, which in the long run, prompted the executions. Profoundly held strict convictions, and the notions of the day likewise helped drive the functions forward.

Widespread panic could help clarify the baffling difficulty of the town's young ladies. Seeing companions displays, certain unexplained practices may have prompted different young ladies to accept that they, as well, were enduring similar side effects. Others recommend that the genuine reason for the Salem witch preliminaries was a long-standing quarrel between various families in Salem Town. The little network was emphatically isolated into various gatherings who battled with one another for strength inside the town. It is conceivable that the guardians of the best young ladies controlled the circumstance to eliminate contradicting powers inside the city.

Different hypotheses have been proposed too. Some have hypothesized that the residents had been harmed by eating a lot of rotten rye, which contains a substance that can cause fantasies and sporadic conduct. Still, others have recommended that maybe the distressed young ladies delighted in the Force they held over the whole town since others would effectively abstain from having an accusatory finger projected toward them. Notwithstanding the reason, the delirium encompassing the preliminaries proceeded into the following year, yet inevitably arrived at a resolution in May of 1693.

Twenty individuals had lost their lives, and Salem Town had perpetually procured its imprint in the set of experiences books.

CHAPTER SIX

NECRONOMICON: THE BOOK OF THE DEAD

Crafted by H.P. Lovecraft has affected innumerable people; we observe this impact today in the enormous loathsomeness classification, however, with sickening dread, just as in a wide range of peculiar fiction. One of his most widespread thoughts was the Necronomicon, an anecdotal grimoire that includes a wide range of dull ceremonies, enchantment, and bizarre sciences. Presently there is the conviction that a Necronomicon may have once existed, and it was deciphered and distributed by Lovecraft. Even though this may not be valid, a great deal of it comes down to Lovecraft himself and how charming the thought was to other people.

There was a ton of history and legend encompassing this specific grimoire, more so than a portion of Lovecraft's other work. He was likewise a genuinely enormous defender of a shared universe, urging different creators to develop his work on the off chance that they saw potential. So when you have these numerous creators referencing a sure thought for this situation, the Necronomicon, you nearly get the inclination that this thought was more likely than not genuine or possibly established in some truth. Furthermore, I surmise the degree of puzzle and vulnerability is why the Necronomicon was utilized by so many, even in current work that doesn't integrate with Lovecraft's mythos.

The proprietor of the Book is a character named Abdul Al Hazarat, whom Lovecraft alludes to as the crazed Bedouin. Al

Hazarat is first to notice quite a while before the dog in the story, The Anonymous City.

Be that as it may, his relationship to the Necronomicon is something we could find later when he was asked where he drew his motivation; Lovecraft essentially furnished the most Lovecraft response. He said it came to him in one he had always wanted, and at this point, we realize that his fantasies and bad dreams were bizarre, no doubt.

He expresses that the name Necronomicon was interpreted by the Greeks to mean a picture of the law of the dead writers then, along these lines followed, have interpreted it to represent a wide range of things from the Book of Laws of the Dead to the Book of names of the dead and even Book of words killed. So what we can sum up from this on an extremely fundamental level is that the Necronomicon was intended to contain data about the dead and the laws that encompassed them, which is very like the enchanted act of sorcery, in premise, yet additionally in the name.

With how puzzling the Necronomicon was in 1927, Lovecraft composed a short piece named The Historical backdrop of the Necronomicon, which wasn't distributed until after his passing. Yet, this piece gives us some extra history and setting. We discover that the Book was initially called Al Assif, alluding to its Arabic cause. The term Al Assif is what Lovecraft characterized as that nighttime sound expected to be the yelling of evil presences. So we positively get the possibility that this Book isn't a signal of bliss and rainbows. It's a lot more obscure and odious.

The Book was composed by Abdul Al Hazarat, whom we referenced prior, yet we didn't specify that he revered Cthulu. Al Hazarat was initially from Yemen, yet it wasn't until he visited Memphis, Egypt, that the thought for the Book started in Memphis.

He ran over the remnants of Babylon and the underground insider facts of the city where he would find the anonymous city. He, at that point, spent the remainder of his daily routine experience in Damascus, what we would perceive as advanced Syria.

In a matter of seconds before his strange vanishing in the year 738, he composed Al Asif, the Necronomicon.

The Book started to circle among thinkers for the following 200 or so years, and in the year 950, it was interpreted by the Greek logician Theodorus Pilates. Also, given the name the Necronomicon, this variant of the Necronomicon was said to impact numerous people into submitting acts so horrible they could scarcely be referenced. Furthermore, that is the reason the Book was signed in the year 1050 by the patriarch of Constantinople.

After this, the Book wasn't generally referenced, and when it was, it was done stealthily to evade any undesirable consideration from those answerable for attempting to delete it from presence.

The Book would then be interpreted from Greek to Latin by a Danish researcher in 1228. The Pope would restrict this release. However, it kept reemerging in other European nations as far as possible until the seventeenth century. Lovecraft states that there are just five duplicates of the first deciphered Necronomicon held in five establishments around the world, and these are the following the English History Historical center in London, the Bibliotheque Nacionale de France, the Weiden, a Library of Harvard College in Cambridge, Massachusetts, the College of Buenos Aires in Argentina.

The last is in Lovecraft's anecdotal town of Arka, Massachusetts, in the Miska Tonic College, which also possesses the Latin interpretation. Presently there are different duplicates of the Book available for use, yet these duplicates were duplicates of copies. So how natural the substance is, we don't generally have the foggiest idea. These duplicates were generally in possession of private people, so they weren't simple nor modest to get it together. So back story aside, I'm sure the inquiry that the vast majority of you need to be addressed is what is in the Book to make it so untouchable, so dim, that every individual who peruses it endures an offensive end.

We realize the Book was composed by somebody who adored the senior divine beings. So as you can envision, they make up a significant enormous aspect of what's within the Necronomicon.

It's brimming with bizarre images and confidential information we can't generally comprehend. Furthermore, its substance goes from stories to customs and a wide range of weird science. In the story, the thing on the doorstep of the Book contains a recipe for one to move their awareness. The Dunwich frightfulness contains a serenade that can gather your considerations, and there are more than a couple of customs that can call gods and a wide range of animals from Lovecraft's universe in Marked. As the name recommends, a part is also given to reviving the dead. Perhaps the most straightforward approach to depict the Necronomicon is as a reference book to everything Lovecraft conceded. It's an exceptionally bizarre reference book that has a propensity for executing any individual who understands it, yet a reference book in any case.

It's likewise an itemized history of what earth may have been similar to ages prior when it was managed and possessed by animals and elements that we can't start to envision. I think what I like most is regardless of the various occasions Love- craft refers to the Book and his accounts; he doesn't generally portray the substance or the appearance in incredible detail. So it remains genuinely secretive, which we don't generally observe many these days with everything being coddled to us.

The main thing we truly know is that it's a calfskin book limited by metal, and still, at the end of the day, it's purposefully mistitled now and again to keep it covered up on display. This thought of having the option to peruse the Necronomicon without knowing makes an entirely different awful idea. The fixation of the Necronomicon, outside of fiction that I referenced, that this trick is no embellishment, there have been. Still, each trusts it to be genuine, and the number of fabrications and odd stories throughout the years bewilders me.

Lovecraft regularly gets letters from fans getting some information about the Book's validity, to which he guaranteed it was simply anecdotal. This didn't prevent a few people from posting the Necronomicon available to be purchased in nearby book shops, just as making sections for the book and library indexes, in any event, going as far as to state the Vatican library had a duplicate themselves.

However, we can put a large portion of this down to cheerful jokesters and some insane individuals.

As the fixation continued filling in 1970, a book named a Necronomicon was distributed by a writer under the alias Simon. It would later be called Simon Necronomicon.

The Book doesn't generally connect to Lovecraft's work but asserts that it impacted them depending on Sumerian folklore. This unquestionably obscured the lines between fiction and reality, with bookselling more than 800000 duplicates starting in 2006.

So it seems a considerable lot of Lovecraft fans were interested enough by the reason to peruse further. It could be because this Book showcased some pretty over-the-top cases; for example, It might be the most hazardous dark Book in the Western world.

In any case, its prosperity implied that three extra volumes were distributed, and I think about why not if individuals needed it.

The significant accomplishment of Simon's Necronomicon prompted the distribution of the records in 1998, which planned to demonstrate that the Book was, in reality, a work of fiction, inspecting only Simon's rendition of the Necronomicon, yet the many dark forms that continued in its prosperity.

Regardless of whether you accept the Necronomicon is genuine. I comprehend the Book's allure in an anecdotal setting and why it would pull in so many kinds of individuals.

CHAPTER SEVEN

WHO IS BAPHOMET?

With the top of a goat in the body of a man, Baphomet stays one of the most dubious gods ever to show up. Frequently mistaken for Satan and a dull history, the goat-headed man is a puzzle that goes back several years. However, the historical backdrop of Baphomet is known to have started with the Knights of the Knight.

It is imagined that the animal has its beginnings in different religions. Baphomet originally came to control in the mid-fourteenth century with the Knights of the Knight. He was a divinity that was incredibly dubious, mainly since it is likely that he has his underlying foundations in Islamic or potentially Egyptian religion. The course of events of bathymetry development is still somewhat indistinct. However, it is as yet conceivable to get an overall thought of the motivation behind divinity. The prior notice of Baphomet, the principal authentic record of Baphomet, originates from a letter composed by a crusader in 1098.

In the letter, he clarifies that the adversaries of the Crusaders could regularly be heard calling Baphomet. There is likewise a record that says the mosques were called Buff Meriuz.

These associations propose that the word Baphomet may have been an error of the name Muhammad if Baphomet is undoubtedly an error of Muhammad. It would clarify why he is viewed as an evil substance by numerous individuals today. This would infer that by venerating Baphomet, the Knights of the Knight were receiving Islamic practices, wrongdoing that would not be disregarded by the Catholic Church to genuinely comprehend the elements at work behind the production of Baphomet. It is critical to ponder the Knights of the Knight and the Campaigns.

The Knights of the Knights were one of the most gifted gatherings of champions. They battled the Campaigns. These missions, which were pointed toward recovering the Heavenly Land from Muslim guidelines, placed the Knights Knights in the Center East for a long while.

During these years, they communicated with individuals who trusted in Islamic lessons. This is the place it is accepted that they initially interacted with Baphomet when the Knights Knights occupied the fight with the soldiers of the Islamic powers. Records show that they frequently heard their adversaries shout to Baphomet before dashing into the battle. In any case, it is imagined that they were yelling at Muhammad, the Islamic prophet. There are a few gossipy tidbits that the Knights of the Knights embraced Baphomet as a symbol and started adoring it abroad.

There are likewise hypotheses, in any case, that the Knights Knights never embraced Islamic practices and were improperly blamed. Ruler Phillip, the fourth of France, blames the Knights for the Knights.

After the holy wars, the Knights of the Knights were one of early Europe's most well-known and ground-breaking bunches. As much as 90% of their gathering involved noncombatants that were answerable for framing a money-related association that could have, in all likelihood, been one of the primary worldwide partnerships to be shaped.

Lord Philip the Fourth. Be that as it may, this represented an issue for Ruler Philip, the fourth of France, after the finish of his nation's battle with England. He was owing debtors to the Knight and wasn't sure he would have the option to think of the cash to reimburse the gathering.

Nonetheless, he would not like to hazard not paying because overlooking the obligation could bring about a military overthrow by the Knights. Instead, he thought of another approach to escape paying in 137 Lord Phillip; the fourth blamed numerous Knights of the Knight for venerating Baphomet and violations like spitting on the cross.

The Knights were tormented until they concocted an admission to the violations, a significant number of them counterfeit, and were then singed at stake. Practically the entirety of the knights confessed to adoring Baphomet; however, inquisitively enough, none of them can concede to what this new icon resembled. This persuaded Ruler Philip, the fourth, to blame the Knights Knight for receiving Islamic practices to cause a frenzy among people in general and dispose of his obligation without such a large number of inquiries being posed. Potential associations with Banebdjedet. Additionally, the individuals accept that the Egyptian God Banebdjedet might have incompletely roused Baphomet, which is somewhat because of the closeness in appearance between the two Banebdjedet is frequently depicted as a slam God, which would have made it genuinely simple to change him into a goat.

Furthermore, Banebdjedet is known to be a Divine being that was regularly searched for his intelligence, a quality that Baphomet would acquire a few centuries later. Baphomet changed in the nineteenth century.

In 1818, Baphomet showed up again when he was found by Joseph Frei, who ravon him, or Bergdoll, who investigated the God and his association with the Knights in an exposition named Finding of the Riddle of Baphomet, by which the Knights, similar to the Gnostics and their battles are indicted for dereliction, of excessive admiration and good debasement by their landmarks.

The article inspects the picture of Baphomet in the yard that encompassed the Knights and the possible downfall that happened to them; accordingly, he would have liked to dishonor the notoriety of the Knights Knight and their artistry work and the Freemasons alongside them.

In any case, there were additionally individuals who challenged his discoveries. Opponent scholars thought cultists had faked almost the pictures. Iliff was Leevi gave Baphomet a face in 1850. Iliff is Leevi remembered Baphomet for a two-volume clique distribution known as Doctrine and the Customs of High Wizardry. In this distribution, he incorporated a hand-drawn portrayal of Baphomet that would turn into a characterizing picture of the animal. His image portrayed a humanoid animal with a goat head and ladies' bosoms. The Baphomet appeared to have a massive pair of wings, horns, a pentagram on his temple, and a drawn portrayal of Baphomet.

This Baphomet accompanied a complicated portrayal of what the picture spoke to in the mysterious. The indication of the pentagram was on its temple, which will likewise contain the Jewish letters of Leviathan. His hands structure the image of the weird and highlight the two moons, the white moon of the chest and the dark moon of Jabarah.

He was also given the fire of insight and showed that his spirit was above the issue, although he was attached to the earth.

Additionally, imagery of unceasing life that remained instead of private parts and portrayal of water, the air, and humankind's quest for the mysterious sciences. Even though Iliff was a portrayal of Baphomet doesn't have any conspicuous associations with the Baphomet depictions recorded at the preliminary of the Knights of the Knight. It is conceivable that his motivation for the picture originated from the peculiar difficult work that was known to be available in the Knight's chapels. There is additionally an intriguing association with the Egyptian divinity Banebdjedet because Levi considered his picture the gold of Méndez.

This is potentially an explanation behind why the Baphomet of Levi has numerous distinctions from the Baphomet of the Knights of the Knight clan.

The inception of the legend, Although there are as yet numerous inquiries that encompass the riddle of Baphomet, it generally concurs that the figure was concocted as a method of blaming Christians for changing over to Islam. The disgrace that the figure increased through the allegations leveled at the Knights of the Knights would bring greater interest in the divinity and theory regarding the animal's potential powers. This shows that the

Baphomet that is loved today was generally affected by the craving to rediscover a potentially enchanted god that figured out how to endure the spread of Christianity.

This is likely why the Baphomet picture has next to no similarity to the symbol depicted by the Knights during their torment and preliminaries.

CHAPTER EIGHT

KRAMPUS: THE EVIL SANTA

It was the previous night of Christmas, and with his folks and kin sleeping soundly in their beds, little Timmy chose to sneak to the first floor and open his presents early. He was filled with energy as he opened everything. However, when he finally got to his gift, Timmy was left peering down at a chilly, rigid piece of coal. The room went cold, and he could hear the shaking of chains behind him. This year, there would be no visit from Santa Clause. The individuals who get into mischief may be welcomed by the shadow of St. Nicholas, the evil presence of Christmas. Krampus.

To many of us, Christmas implies a period of euphoria, fellowship, and family; however, if we're being straightforward as children, it means no school and a lot of presents. There are those, anyway, tragic enough to encounter the dark side of Christmas.

The individuals who never got their visit from Santa Clause act mischievously, and you will be on Santer's insidious rundown. Yet, imagine a scenario in which that rundown was something beyond acting mischievously to youngsters. Imagine a scenario where that rundown was planned for another person. There's nothing similar to stories of an evil presence who suffocates, eats, and hauls youngsters off to hellfire to truly get you into the Christmas disposition.

Jokes aside, Krampus is one of my undisputed top choices. Accounts of Krampus have shown up all through Focal Europe as far back as the pre-Christian high convention. This region covers a large group of nations from Austria, Germany, and Switzerland to parts of France, northern Italy, the Czech Republic, and Slovenia.

Present-day stories portray him as the not-all-that-agreeable buddy of Holy person Nicholas or Santa Clause Claus, who rebuffs the ineffectively carried on. At the same time, St. Nicholas remunerates acceptable individuals. In any case, it might not have consistently been that way while talking about Krampus. Two specific timeframes give us various stories—the underlying time of agnostic custom and the period after the Christian convention. We genuinely don't think much about his soonest inception because most agnostic traditions were either overlooked or retained in Christian rituals. The most well-known conviction is that Krampus may have started from a horned divinity.

Moreover, we realize this broadens beyond agnostic convictions because horned divine beings have existed in various societies worldwide. There is a similitude between Krampus and the old Greek Sator, both being very unruly and naughty. However, one is more detestable than the other. In senior high German, the word crampon implied Paw, which could allude to a pawed beast.

Yet, much like all that else encompassing his roots, it's all pretty questionable. The nearest association we can draw between Krampus pre and post-Christian snow-capped customs are agnostic celebrations that occurred throughout the colder time of year, like Yule or Winter Solstice. During these celebrations, men would spruce up in covers, and creature hides and march around towns being an aggravation, which is something they do today. Yet, we'll get into that somewhat later. Up until now, there's not been a lot to propose that Krampus ever had anything to do with Christmas or Santa Clause Claus other than showing up at a comparative time in the year in both Austria and Germany; it wasn't unprecedented for people to wear an underhanded cover and make irritation of themselves during occasions, which respected Christian holy people.

This wasn't done as a convention respecting Krampus. All the more so was a pushback against the congregation, which had eliminated these agnostic convictions and traditions. You can, notwithstanding, make the contention that this would be the beginning of what we would find in the years that followed. If we go further back, the nearest thing we have to a source for Krampus originates from a figure referred to in Austria as Perchta. She was referenced quickly by the Siblings Grimm, and the ideal way I can portray her is as a mix of Santa Clause Claus and Krampus.

Instead of having the idea of good and evil appear by two separate substances, culprits are spoken to both the prize and the discipline around midwinter. During what we would allude to as the 12 days of Christmas or the Gala of the Revelation, she would visit youngsters' homes. On the off chance that they were acceptable, they would locate a silver coin in one of their shoes the following morning. Sounds a ton like St. Nicholas, isn't that so?

Supposing they were awful, she would cut open their midsections, eliminate their stomach and guts and fill the cavity with straw and rocks before sewing it shut again. This additionally reached out to any individual who ate something besides meat, fish, or Flame broil during the day of her celebration to represent this duality; she showed up as a delightful lady wearing white and different occasions as a shriveled old witch going with her or gathering of spirits known as the Perchta, who, much the same as Perchta, likewise showed up in two unique structures the excellent Perchta who carried with them favorable luck and the terrible Perchtun who had teeth, tusks, and ponytails not very not quite the same as Krampus himself.

The monstrous Perchtan were utilized to avert spirits and devils in one's home, like Halloween. Be that as it may, in December, this prompted men to take on the appearance of these monstrous Perchtun and go from house to house, driving out insidious spirits in what was known as the Perchtun chuckle or the Perchtan run. The congregation, at that point, considered these to be a show of unethical conduct, attempting to prevent these runs from occurring.

In any case, numerous Austrian townspeople would not consent, while others decided to dress somebody up as a Holy person Nicholas to go with them on these runs as, to some degree, a trade-off. Around the eleventh century, accounts of St. Nicholas started to pick up prevalence, which continued until the sixteenth century when the type of Krampus that we realize today started to show. The congregation secured a fight with the Austrian individuals over the agreement and chose to simply inside and out boycott the Perchtan, presently not ready to surrender completely. The individuals at that point made another animal like the Perch in appearance, yet with a couple of critical changes. This animal would now serve St. Nicholas and be known as Krampus, a bushy horned and huge satanic figure with sharp teeth, extended hooks, and a significantly longer tongue.

Right now, he wasn't viewed as just one of his sort. The Krampus alluded to a race of beasts that showed up during the period. During this period, Christians would observe St. Nicholas; Dec. six was known as St. Nicholas Day. Much like Current Christmas, St. Nicholas would convey presents to the individuals who had been acceptable.

The individuals who were not that great would get a chunk of coal or a twig from the congregation. The possibility of these Krampus figures was, as yet, an image of heathenism; thus, they chose to acclimatize this conviction into their reality winter services. St. Nicholas then matched Krampus. One represents the great and the other fiendishness. He would then become related to the possibility of the Christian friend, and he was offered chains to designate the villain's office by the congregation.

He currently hefted around birch sticks that he would use to beat getting out of hand youngsters on his back. He had a container or a sack that he would toss those underhanded youngsters in a while, hauling them off to hellfire. You may even be suffocated or eaten if you were inadequately acted. The previous night St. Nicholas Day presently became Krampus Night, December fifth, was the day this devil was permitted to wander the roads and towns. At this point, don't Holy person Nicholas give you a twig or a piece of coal. He was just worried about the great kids. The discipline of the rest tumbled to Krampus. It was essential for the congregation to incorporate thoughts and customs from different societies into their own when endeavoring to change over those from alternate confidence.

Furthermore, it bodes well. Simply turning up close to home and instructing them to quit having confidence in what they do because they go into damnation typically inspires a negative response. Giving them a shared conviction in your convictions is considerably more viable. In this situation, it was all the more so the Austrian individuals who adjusted their beliefs into something more acceptable to the congregation.

Thus, the holy person Nicholas and Krampus's account is a genuine case of how a barbarian conviction was incorporated. Notwithstanding the significant contrasts, the convention of St. Nicholas Day experienced a significant severe move because of this going from St. Nicholas, leaving you a twig, maybe, inadequately carried on to being hauled off to damnation by this goliath devil goat beast. If you were fortunate, perhaps you'd be eaten or suffocated in a lake—a remarkable apparent move.

By the sixteenth century, accounts of St. Nicholas started to be supplanted; he currently became Santa Clause Claus, getting from his Dutch name, Sinterklaas, or Father Christmas. If you live in the UK, accounts of Krampus remain to a great extent, the equivalent. Also, December fifth was considered a Krampus night in numerous nations, with Christmas commended on the 25th.

It's normal to move Krampus night to Christ- mas Eve for that outside of the High Locale. Moreover, you may see this in different stories and motion pictures, regardless of these festivals and celebrations occurring toward the beginning of December.

These festivals can fluctuate contingent on the locale. They frequently include wearing a wooden cover, sprucing up in hiding, and endeavoring to look as frightening as expected.

In certain towns, it's more entertaining; in others, it's marginally more terrifying. Be that as it may's, everything generally was done with great fun.

The most mainstream of these customs is the Kampusch Snicker or the Krampus run, equivalent to the Perchtun giggle. Gatherings of individuals take on the appearance of Krampus wearing enormous chimes so they can be heard as they meander the roads in packs, joined by a Holy person Nicholas. What they do precisely relies upon how they're feeling. Some panic youngsters and passers-by. Some toss snow at them, and others whip them around the rear of the leg.

At that point, you have the individuals who visit houses present, and in return, they're given schnapps and cognac. So it's a practically grown-up stunt or treating. Furthermore, it's additionally a very decent reason to stroll around being a gigantic douche for a day in parts of Austria; Twiggs would be painted gold and gone outlasting through the year as an update for youngsters to carry on in the eighteen hundreds, Krampus could be found on welcome cards, postcards and on the coverings of sweets.

These portrayals were somewhat odd and frequently very tacky. They highlight Krampus as an all the more evil figure with a sexual connotation. What's more, this stems from those in enormous urban areas never truly observing these customs. All they needed to pass by was the congregation's expression, which likened Krampus to the fiend regarding his story.

These pictures do bode well. However, it's not hard to envision why some wouldn't discover them reasonably. It's also why they've gone from alarming to more silly to interest a bigger crowd throughout the long term.

It's ideal to see that these celebrations and Krampus runs happen today, not simply in towns and urban communities inside Austria and Germany, but all around the globe, in any event, springing up in parts of North America.

No doubtful accounts of Krampus and those originating before him have a dull tone. In any case, to state that he's simply shrewd doesn't generally recount the entire story.

Before they were Christianized, the Perchtan filled in as defensive spirits, and Krampus just indeed came to St. Nicholas, his partner, as an approach to keep these customs alive.

And still, at the end of the day, he rebuffs the individual's considered merits. He doesn't submit demonstrations of evil against the guiltless; consequently, he can be viewed as speaking to a vital malevolence.

This entire display was and still is a period of fun and articulation for some. Indeed, even today, families take their kids to these functions and celebrations. To them, Krampus is all the more a Disney miscreant than a scary evil story. Krampus and the Holy person Nicholas speak to our unique nature.

We can be acceptable, and we can be malevolent. Yet, with the goal for society to work, you need a motivating force for the tremendous ramifications of the awful, regardless of whether that is as a furry devilish goat beast.

CHAPTER NINE

CAIN: CHILD OF SATAN AND SERPENT SEED HYPOTHESIS

One of the most dubious thoughts that have been shaped on the accounts of the Good Book is the seven-seed hypothesis or the two-seed mind the assumption that seems to have originated from early Gnostic compositions, most remarkably the Good news of Philip, composed at some point in the third century.

This vile dad hypothesis gives an elective plan for the fall of man and what has very restricted proof to help it, as I would see it, is a severe clear, intriguing plan to consider.

Before we start, let me just put out a disclaimer that this isn't the hypothesis that I fundamentally buy into, it is only a thought proposed by the Gnostic writings, writers of different midrash, and other American strict pioneers, most prominently the evangelist William M Branham. Generally, the idea has been dismissed by numerous standard Christian scholars and doesn't hold a lot of weight once you dissect it. Be that as it may, how about we plunge into it for ourselves?

Seven seed thought, which I'm sure you've speculated from the title, is the possibility that Cain is the child of the snake in the Nursery of Eden and that of Adam as ordinarily accepted. This paints Eve as having been faithless to Adam and that someplace during her time in the Nursery of Eden, she was enticed by the snake and conveyed his child, a kid who might become a lord. If Adam knew about her disloyalty is obscure. However, some Midrash journalists trusted him to be uninformed of current realities, given that he proceeds to cause a stir similarly as he raised Abel while never appearing to treat him unexpectedly, nor any impassion towards Eve from that point. Where must midrashic look legitimize this hypothesis is by the distinction in conduct and disposition between Cain and Abel?

You'll see that where Abel is benevolent in that he wishes to forfeit something imperative to God, Cain is undeniably more economical and looks to lose to what he doesn't require any longer. The Good Book reveals to us now Abel kept groups and Cain needed the dirt. Throughout, the opportunity arrived for a portion of the products of the land as a contribution to the Ruler, and Abel likewise forwarded contribution fat parts from a bit of the firstborn of his rush.

The Master approves of Abel and his contribution, yet he doesn't look with favor on Cain and his gift. So Cain was angry, and his face was depressed. Anybody perusing the Holy book would comprehend that the distinction in how God treats them is in connection to how commendable their penance is, where Abel gave got something essential to him, that being the primary conceived of his run and related fat parts, Cain gives him products of the dirt. Furthermore, there are ramifications here: Cain's penance was on the miserly side by correlation.

It becomes evident that God favors evil; however, he seems to disregard Cain. The seven seed hypothesis, in any case, endeavors to legitimize Cain being the child of the snake by proposing that God didn't give Cain a similar thankfulness, not because he was disillusioned in his penance, but since he detested Cain since Cain was the result of the Snakes, his human adversary, Satan.

Usually, God realizes every one of that has occurred. Thus he would subsequently have known about Eve's illicit relationship. Besides, he will likewise understand that, again, Satan has had the option to degenerate something he adored. We realize this is Satan's definitive goal, all things considered, and that all he does is degenerate man since he realizes this is presumably one of the main ways he's ready to hurt God. Usually, Satan detests men. Thus he would do anything in his capacity to cut them down. However, by enticing Eve, he gets the opportunity to demonstrate hatred for her and Adam. Still, on the other hand, he's ready to leave a lasting imprint upon the world by utilizing his posterity to spread his wrongdoing. Another thought here, once more unverified, is that God didn't remove Adam and Eve since the snake enticed them but since Eve had lain with it. I accept this is a test since it further strengthens an early Christian thought that ladies are the foundation of all insidious and that ladies are liable for the defeat of men.

There's likewise the possibility that while Scott knew about Eve's unfaithfulness and wrongness of Cain, God has Cain's leniency; we continued to let him know in the Good Book; for what reason would you say you are irate? For what reason is your face discouraged? On the off chance that you make the wisest decision, will you not be acknowledged? However, sin is hunching at your entryway if you don't make the right decision. It wants to have you, yet you should control it. So regardless of his parentage and notwithstanding being the child of the snake, God assumes the best about Cain.

He attempts to improve himself into a man and still tries to show him the correct way rather than simply projecting him out as it happens or, more terribly, executing him. He looks to exhibit the right way and gives him direction in a most sustaining manner, maybe unquestionably more than he merited, given his more obscure expectations.

We see similar dull aims show when Cain executes Abel and plays out the absolute first homicide; some midrash and early Gnostic works endeavor to nail this homicide to the inalienable evilness of Cain not because he was simply desirous of his sibling. In this hypothesis, Cain slaughters Abel since it is, in a real sense, in his blood. He is the child of the villain. Thus he usually would have evil in him, which makes him more slanted to brutality. We, at that point, see Cain Pacita lie to God when asked where Abel is. Out of nowhere, the line 'Am I my sibling's attendant?' takes on a different importance, for Cain's insidious streak is well and genuinely stirred. Cain looks to attempt to trick God, and while this may probably be his naivety in that, he wants to deceive the Master or perhaps endeavors to conceal his blameworthy activities. It seems like something Satan would attempt to do.

Cain's attempt to deceive God shows that he can't quit erring. Presently they began. Moreover, he doesn't show any regret here for murdering his sibling and appears to be undeniably more worried about the discipline he suffers, which is to meander the land as an eager soul. The Holy book lets us know this; the Ruler stated, "what have you done? Tune in; your sibling's blood shouts out to me from the beginning. Presently you're under a revile and driven from the beginning to open its mouth to get your sibling's blood from your hand when you tilled the fields. It will, at this point, don't yield its harvests for you. You will be an eager drifter on the earth". The way that Stick shows little respect for killing his sibling and appears to be undeniably more worried about himself is assuredly a mischievous and unwanted character attribute.

In any case, is this enough to recommend that this makes him the child of Satan? Professors in this Snake seed hypothesis would contend that the primary other men at present at that point, Adam and Abel, didn't show a similar devilishness. Thus Cain couldn't have been identified with them since he's completely different in his reasoning and conduct. Past this, there isn't much to help this hypothesis utilizing this contention alone. Cain is nothing similar to Adam and Abel, given that he's fit for homicide; however, we don't see Adam and Abel tried similarly.

So who knows whether they would have acted likewise had they been snuffed by God? The most eminent devotee of this hypothesis was the evangelist William Branham, who made this a stride further and accepted that since Eve had lain with the snake, this put each other lady brought into the world after Eve in a perpetual condition of wrongdoing. So they also conveyed the seed of the villain.

To him and other people who accept this hypothesis, it portrays everything being equal. Because the absolute first lady turned out to be the absolute first lady to undermine her companion, all ladies were slanted to do likewise.

He likewise accepts that there were two separate fatalities on the planet, those that were the equitable relatives of Adam and the individuals who were the wise relatives of Cain. Those that plummeted from Adam were, obviously, God- Dreading and looked to do great on the planet; those that were slid from Cain were fiendish, however, not because they were more disposed to murder or cheat or do any evil things like that. No. As per Branham, they were likewise more slanted to examine science and teach themselves past the requirements of religion. Without a doubt, it appears Branham shows instruction itself as wrongdoing since it was something of a snare utilized by Satan to cloud the lessons in the Book of scriptures and the expression of God. To him, training and ladies were the two most significant components that could lead a man into debasement.

Although this isn't the least of his strange thoughts, he additionally accepted that the snake, having laid down with Eve, was the missing connection between the chimpanzee and man. Another study by different allies of the snake seed hypothesis is that the Jews were the relatives of Adam and Seth with the Knights. A migrant clan in old Israel were the relatives of the Ruler. Past this, there isn't a lot to help this hypothesis. Different midrashic have attempted to detail the function itself, whereby it's been informed that the snake tricked Eve away from Adam while he was dozing and had his way with her.

Different understandings accept that Adam was conscious of the function and couldn't prevent Eve from meandering into the Snakes curls. Others assume that Eve was deceived or disagreed with the snake's enticement. However, the predominant hypothesis is that Eve eagerly lay with the seven, and we got a youngster.

In the Lord James' rendition of the Book of scriptures, Beginning 315 shows us the discipline God gives the snake of the healer to Adam and Eve have eaten from the tree of information on tremendous and malevolence.

He says, "And I will put hatred among the lady and between thy seed and her seed." Here, God is likely alluding to their posterity when he discusses seed and states there will consistently be aggression among men and specific. Be that as it may, it is here with a hypothesis being referred to gets its namesake as the two-seed hypothesis, where adherents consider seeds to be this case, as strict as in the seed inside Satan and his seed, which presently lay inside eve. The most tricky thing about this entire hypothesis is that half of us living on the planet is, in the real sense, relatives of Satan.

While once more, this isn't a sound rationale, it may be the main thing from this hypothesis that would bode well. The entire theory, however, welcomes some risky inquiries and philosophical Catch-22s. If this is valid, that would suggest that evil presences can mate with people, as well, and produce posterity. On the off chance that not, and Satan is the one in particular who has this capacity, at that point, what are the odds of him doing it again?

Consider it on the off chance that he had the option to do it directly under the nose of God in his one-of-a-kind nursery. Is it accurate that we are relied upon to accept that he had never tried to do it again on earth, where he had far simpler access and maybe far fewer results? On the off chance that this hypothesis is to be accepted, at that point, Satan has presumably been laying down with ladies for a considerable number of years and topping off the world with his loathsome produce.

To numerous devotees, the fall of man is pretty highly contrasting. The fall is about rebellion against God, not because Eve had a nervy excursion. I'm almost sure the creators of the Book of scriptures would have been quick to specify this if that was the situation expressly. Moreover, the general agreement is that Cain was only juvenile in not having the option to have his feelings and not innately evil since he was the perfect example of insidious Satan. Furthermore, by and by, I accept that the more you gaze at something, the almost sure you are to devise an elective thought, something that probably won't have been the first creator's expectation.

CHAPTER TEN

EVIDENCE ABOUT EGYPTIAN PHARAOHS BEING ALIENS

Much has been said about incredible landmarks around the globe that are so radiant in their structures that it boggles the psyche how the people of old constructed them. As per a few scholars, individuals didn't assemble them. In any case, outsiders plunged from the skies in what some have called monster Saucer formed pontoons. Also, it was those creatures that manufactured the structures. If they had not manufactured them at that point, coordinate the development. That is how a pyramid could be made. Sitting at true north, state the scholars, they go above and beyond to reveal to us that the pharaohs were outsiders, human half and halves sound very fantastical.

Yet, what's driving some to make these cases? Is there any proof whatsoever? We should investigate why a few people accept this. As you may have found in our different shows on the pyramids, to certain Egyptologists, the subject of how the pyramids were manufactured remains covered in the riddle. We're not just discussing the hard work of moving many stones, hauling them over the land, and afterward, up the establishment. However, the supreme accuracy concerning exactly how they lie, the way that the pyramids of Giza sit true north, ought to be dumbfounding to pretty much anybody, not simply trick scholars. At the same time, other people who have examined the structure demand that this incredible landmark is worked to mirror the elements of our planet.

There are pundits of this hypothesis, and they express that if you mix the numbers enough, you can get the outcomes. It would help if you accommodated your theory. In any case, with the pyramids being so staggeringly magnificent, it's justifiable that a few people imagine that people had some assistance from something not of this world, marginally more sensible, yet simultaneously outside of the standard. Scholars have their speculation, saying it wasn't outsiders that accomplished the work. However, preceding the old Egyptians, another serious human advancement existed on Earth that had given their insight to them before we went to the outsider half-breed pharaohs.

How about we take a gander at some different reasons why a specific fragment of the general population accepts outsiders came rational left and afterward were loved as divine beings by old civic establishments. First, we have the Moai of Easter Island and the goliath stone heads that absolutely couldn't have been difficult to raise. There's a lot of proof that it was feasible for the Moai to assemble these sculptures. However, there are as yet those that express that they were inherent to the state of the outsiders who helped in their development.

At that point, there's the old Bolivian sanctuary, Panther Punku, which was worked with stones weighing more than 100 tons. Indeed, even today, researchers are contradictory concerning how people moved them. The rocks in the sanctuary fit together like an interlocking riddle, which would have implied that those developers needed a significant comprehension of calculation and artistry. Not just that, the unfathomably complicated improvements in the stones are such exceptional specialists don't generally have the foggiest idea of how they figured out how to make them with such fundamental apparatuses.

Tests on mummies have demonstrated that individuals in the region routinely devoured stimulating plants. To certain scholars, this was their method of interfacing with a different universe, which may help clarify their splendid motivation.

We won't experience all the incredible marvels on this planet Earth. However, numerous recorded destinations boggle the brain. Take, for instance, Stonehenge in the U.K., or again the sanctuaries of Vijayanagara in India that appear to have outsider-looking considers and items cut along with the stonework. We are in no way, shape, or form endeavoring to influence you into believing that since people in the past indicated that they could do fantastic things, that implies that they had help from outsiders.

Yet, we're just saying that this is a motivation behind why a few people accept this may have occurred. Back to the Egyptians. Have you ever observed an image of Pharaoh Akhenaten, the dad of Lord Tut, who was said to have been the living encapsulation of the sun-oriented God and kicked the bucket around 1336 BC? Many residual relics portray what Akhenaten resembled. What's more, guess what? He has an extended head, much like the typical dark outsider.

You can discover one stone cutting of him revering the circle of the sun known as the Atin with the light emissions radiating down on him. Taking a gander at this, however, with these extended heads looking an outsider instead as if you didn't know better, you might feel that the great circle was a spaceship, some flying saucer. This is since quite a while ago shot. What's more, if you read more about antiquated human advancements, you'll see that portraying individuals with prolonged heads happened a ton, from the Australian Natives to the Mayans to numerous different spots.

Some have recommended that this may have been because they had massive heads, a slander called Macrocephaly, which essentially implies a giant head in antiquated Greek. This may have been the consequence of inbreeding or ailment that prompted the variation from the norm. It might have likewise been done deliberately. Cranial misshapen may have additionally been an exceptionally agonizing method, something the offspring of good birth needed to experience to make them look dissimilar to their ordinary people.

The hypothesis is that it offered pioneers to be incredible glory.

Whatever the explanation, there's a great deal of proof of antiquated individuals having these enormous heads everywhere in the world. A few people would have you accept that these individuals were outsider mixtures or, if nothing else, molded to resemble the extraordinary things that originated from the sky. There's no genuine strong proof for this, however. It's a simple theory or more like a dream. Concerning the incomparable Akhenaten, did he truly have a severe head? His mummy would disclose this to us, yet we'll get around to that soon.

At that point, there are the dreams of the English newspaper press who have, on occasion, not let the realities impede advising a decent story. In 2016, a portion of the sensationalist newspapers distributed an article about an old Egyptian coin on Earth; if you see it, there's no uncertainty that one side depicts the prolonged top of a dark outsider. The issue with this is that the main proof of the genuine coin was a line that revealed to us the antique was found by a gathering of individuals who shot at redesigning a house in southern Egypt.

We searched for more data on this strange gathering of renovators and couldn't discover anything. However, we found coin specialists discussing the outsider head bit of money. What's more, they said this. A little exploration uncovered that it's not so much a genuine curio yet an intensely corrected or Photoshopped picture of an authentic Roman emblem in the popular assortment in Paris. PC researcher Ralph Bulow revealed the scam. So much for dependable news sources.

We found another questionable source disclosing to us that a DNA trial of Egyptian mummies uncovered a quality called CXPAC-5, which we're told is liable for the structure of the frontal cortex, the thinking part about the cerebrum. Eight out of nine mummies didn't contain this, yet the mummy of Pharaoh Akhenaten did. The article, at that point, hops to the end that outsiders, more likely than not, planted this in the pharaoh. The blog entry discloses that it's bizarre to discover five in the mummy of Akhenaten since he kicked the bucket at age 45, and it just shows up in many more established individuals.

Akhenaten appeared to have a severe mind that said we can locate nobody, yet outsider fans discussing it. Indeed, there are no connections prompting the alleged investigation that reveals to us the pharaoh may have been connected in some way or another to outsiders due to the presence of this quality. Researchers are not sure where he was covered in any case, with it being suspected that he may have been let go in Cavern 55, a burial place in the Valley of the Rulers in Egypt; one of the skulls discovered there was broadened, however, it's the idea that this was a direct result of a sickness called persistent hydrocephalus.

This essentially implies a lot of liquid on the cerebrum that can mutilate the head. Different specialists state that people with old augmented heads might have been down to other conditions that cause Macrocephaly. In any case, the legitimate specialists discuss if the skull was Akhenaten's. Furthermore, they haven't set forth a hypothesis that outsiders have planted a quality in his mind that made it more prominent or made him cannier.

The outsider adherents indeed associated many undetectable specks with making that story work.

At last, there's the purportedly old Egyptian content called the Tulli Papyrus. You'll discover specific sources saying this contains content that appears as though it discusses UFOs. One interpretation of part of the content peruses in English In the year 22, the third month of winter, 6th hour of the day, the contents of the Place of Life discovered it was a hover of fire coming in the sky. Another part peruses, They were more varied than anything.

They were sparkling in the sky more than the sun to the furthest reaches of the power supports of paradise. Incredible was the situation of the fire circles. Stunning. That positively seems like it may have been a record of an outsider locating. The main issue is the Tulli Papyrus isn't a bona fide papyrus. It's a record of a supposed report whose source is questionable, best case scenario. Indeed, even some ufologists consider the whole thing a lie, saying somebody was hanged in an old archive and revealed to it was a record of the first.

And afterward, somebody deciphered that, which is about it in something many refer to as the Condon Report, a report by a gathering supported by the U.S. Aviation-based armed forces on the chance of outsider life coming to Earth. This Tulli papyrus was discussed. The specialists composed that it was taken from auxiliary and tertiary sources with no endeavors to confirm unique sources. They likewise said that all such records of UFO sightings passed on from old occasions have become powerless and strange. Until they can be established, they're negligible.

CHAPTER ELEVEN

KUCHISAKE ONNA: THE SLIT-MOUTHED LADY

Kuchisake Onna, or the cut-mouthed lady of the horrible Soul with her face secured with a veil, gazed back at youthful Shiro from the Book of Japanese society stories and legends, and he needed to know more. Who right? For what reason would she say she was brimming with rage, and what was under that cover? Shiro's mom, Heena, was a sincere lady who put stock in the old manners and attempted to give them to her child through stories.

A solid devotee to the Soul, she generally needed Shiro to proceed cautiously on the off chance that he experienced a heavenly. Shiro's dad, Kenichi, was another story. He just had faith in one Soul saké. He would habitually return home alcoholic and affront his better half. He burst through the entryway similarly as Shiro requested that his mom disclose the cut-mouthed lady's narrative to him. Is it true that you are topping Kid's head with those stupid stories? Once more, they're not stupid. As his dad flung the Book over the room, Shiro withdrew to his room.

He realized what it resembled when his dad was temperament and tuned in to the yelling between his folks until he heard the unmistakable sound of an entryway pummel. His dad was not uncertain about becoming inebriated at the bar again and wouldn't be back until late. He couldn't have cared less what his dad said. He knew the spirits his mom cautioned him about were genuine, and he trusted his dad wouldn't experience any on his way to the watering gap. It was late in the moon was high in the sky when Kenichi meandered back from the bar.

He realized it would be another contention when he returned home, and he strolled gradually, cautious not to stagger, he had more than his fill in a woodland way between the bar, and home looked more winding and shadowy than ordinary. As he drew nearer, he saw the weak layout of a lady in the evening glow impeding his way. Heena that you couldn't try and stand by till he returned home to holler at me. There was no reaction from the lady. As Kenichi strolled forward and through his saké obscured eyes, he could gradually observe that this wasn't his significant other. It was a dull-haired lady, her face secured with a cover. Furthermore, she was holding what resembled a bizarrely long pair of scissors.

He was unable to see her face unmistakably. However, he wagers she was lovely under that cover, and unexpectedly he was in no rush to return home. My lovely? The lady asked delicately as Kanichi strolled nearer. Indeed, you are, he said with a grin. Is it accurate to say that you are looking to? The lady gradually emerged, eliminating her veil, and Kanichi whitened with sickening dread underneath the fabric. Her face was disfigured, and her mouth split from ear to ear. In a wound, unnaturally wide smile, my wonderful Kanichi shouted with dismay, going to run with the cut mouth lady who moved unnaturally quickly. In a subsequent, she was on her scissors and her hand, wounding him repeatedly. Kanichi shouts, repeating through the timberland. Be that as it may, nobody was around to hear or consider him to be the wrathful Soul who hauled him away. Indeed, practically nobody Shiro had been viewing from the window, pondering when his dad would return.

He saw him approach the finish of the way, his route impeded by a lady. He saw his dad turn and run the glimmer of enormous scissors in the twilight, and he realized his dad would not be getting back. He attempted to tell his mom what had occurred, yet she got over him. Kanichi was famously temperamental, and she demanded he'd advance home inevitably. Be that as it may, his days passed with no indication of the man. Their house was long-loaded up with aunties and cousins offering their feelings. Unmistakably, he was questionable. Flushed spouse had run off and forsaken the family. Any time Shiro attempted to raise what he had seen, he was advised to be tranquil and not annoyed by his mom. However, he realized the cut-mouthed lady was out there, and she had removed his dad. Also, Shiro was resolved to illuminate the secret.

A long time passed, and Shiro developed from a kid into a youngster. Although he was occupied with school, he generally made a chance to investigate the legend of the animal that had taken his dad. He never got any nearer to discovering reality, yet he was far from the primary individual inspired by the legend. It wasn't easy to recognize genuine reports of the animal from all individuals making up tales about her. She had shown up in manga, anime, computer games, and enlivened motion pictures. There had even been a progression of thrillers about her named the Cut, Mouthed Lady. Be that as it may, barely any individuals appeared to accept she was anything over a frightening story to be told at day camp or on Web discussions.

Shiro posted on the Web requesting individuals who had experienced the Soul and was stunned when he got one reaction back. It was an older adult living about an hour away after school. He advised his mom he was setting off to the library to contemplate and instead took the transport to the older adult's town. He had been instructed to meet him in the library, and when he showed up, the administrator disclosed that the man was sitting tight for him in the peaceful investigation room.

The room was dull, and the older adult was occupied with perusing a book. He didn't pivot to welcome Shiro close to the kid investigating spirits. Indeed, sir. The Cut mouth lady. Shiro could swear he saw the man shudder as he discussed her. My dad experienced her, and I think she slaughtered him. I'm not astonished she does that to many people who say some unacceptable thing too. It was scarcely more established than you when I experienced her. She asked me for a similar inquiry. She asks everybody, Am I delightful? She's a prostitute under that cover.

Also, if you let her realize you believe that there's no moving endlessly alive. Me, I heard the tales.

I recognized what to state, or so I thought. I gazed at her privilege in the face, that horrendous smile. Furthermore, I disclosed to her I thought she was lovely. What's more, you endure. Shiro inhaled a murmur of alleviation. There was an approach to get away. No doubt, the older adult said with an interruption. However, she needed to know whether I would not joke about this. So she left me with the memory of our experience. The older person put his Book down and gradually turned around. His cheeks were excessive since quite a while ago mended, scars denoting his face, parting his cheeks from ear to ear.

The slit-mouthed lady had denoted the older adult simply like her face. Shiro immediately thanked the older adult for his time and beat a hurried retreat from the library. Who is this lady, and what did she need? Would she slaughter and injure anybody she experienced regardless of what they said? He required the appropriate responses, and he continued exploring. He had to know her root. Be that as it may, he discovered there wasn't only one birthplace. There were many. Everybody assumed the cut mouth lady was the Soul of a lady who'd been unpleasantly injured throughout everyday life and was looking for her retribution. In any case, nobody could concur on what had befallen her. The older person affirmed that she had been frequenting Japan for quite a long time. In any case, legends returned to the Edo time frame, the seventeenth century. A few renditions of the code said she was the spouse or courtesan of an extraordinary samurai who disfigured her when she had an unsanctioned romance. Others said she was the casualty of a dental specialist or specialist who messed up a strategy all over or that she'd been cut by a sentimental opponent who was envious of her magnificence. Others said she wasn't the Soul of a disfigured lady by any stretch of the imagination. He said she was a Yorkie or powerful animal and that the cuts weren't a cut. They were her characteristic mouth, brimming with many sharp teeth that she used to devour any individual who crossed her way. A long time went on, and Shiro never found the appropriate response he was searching for.

There were many extraordinary anecdotes about the animal, and nobody was sure how to endure an involvement in her sound. Some said you needed to give her a blessing. Others noted that regardless of whether she let somebody pass, she would return and murder them later. Before long, Shiro met a young lady, Sakura, and they wedded and had offspring of their own life was occupied. Shiro once in a while had the opportunity to harp on those awful recollections from adolescence, with one exemption the commemoration of his dad's passing. Every year, as the day drew nearer, he got progressively fixated on the Cut mouth lady. He would pore over the books of old stories, searching for pieces of information. His mom had instructed him to let the past go, not to let the spirits frequent him. Yet, he was fixated. His youngsters would come to request that their dad plays with him. However, he would release them away, saying he was occupied. Sakura came to haul him out of his examination, and they fought. Before long, he took a stroll to clear his brain. Possibly he'd get a beverage to bring some relief. The night was fresh and clear as Shiro strolled home from the bar and was happy he had just one drink. He realized Sakura had good intentions and could not hold back from returning home to work things out with her.

Was that her sitting tight for him toward the finish of the way? It wasn't. Shiro's blood ran cold as he perceived the figure hindering his way home. It was a similar lady he had seen each one of those years sooner, hanging tight to his dad. Same white dress, matching dark hair, the same cover over the face, a similar pair of scissors in hand. Furthermore, presently her eyes were fixed immovably on him. Somehow. He was going to find the solutions he was searching for. Am I lovely? Shiro realized nobody endures disapproving of the cut mouth lady, and he addressed yes. He prepared himself as she came up and removed her cover, uncovering her disfigured face. He kept a consistent face, not responding. Some unacceptable responses could spell passing. Am I excellent? She rehashed in a similar, frequented, impartial tone. You look fine, normal, Shiro reacted, trusting this would affect them. Perhaps she didn't need individuals to lie. However, she didn't need them to recognize her disfigurement. The cut-confronted lady didn't react; she just glanced at him curiously. This wasn't a reaction she was ready for, yet she didn't move. She was hanging tight for something else. Shiro ventured into his pocket and scarcely contained a giggle.

More likely, her little girl slipped them into his pocket before he stomped out. On the off chance that he was ravenous, he took them out and put the little desserts on the ground as a contribution. The slit-faced woman tilted her head toward the candy and quickly moved forward and gathered them. That gave Shiro the opportunity he needed to move around her quickly. Toward the end of the path and into the clearing. He'd heard the rustling behind him, but he didn't look back until he was safe at his front door. When he finally turned around, the slit-faced woman was nowhere to be seen, and he felt he had seen the last of her. As Shiro entered his home and embraced his wife and children, he promised he would remember what his mother had taught him today. He would pass down the stories of the spirits to his children and ensure they knew how to escape them. After all, the slit-faced woman was still out there for another terrifying creature that may be lurking in the woods.

CHAPTER TWELVE

MOST CURESED OBJECTS IN THE WORLD

Unpleasant dolls and evil presence boxes maybe two of the items to make this rundown, yet some other cast objects are undeniably more unassuming. A part of these you could undoubtedly go over in regular daily existence without comprehending what you were getting yourself into. The revile seat lethally harmed countless individuals, and its proprietor chose to hang it up until the end of time.

How about we get into reviled objects you certainly don't have any desire to claim?

1. James Senior member's Porsche 550 Spyder - The Porsche 550 Spyder may seem a noteworthy vehicle; however, it's one that we'd suggest appreciating in a good way. The model probably won't be excessively hazardous. However, there's one specific vehicle that is believed to be reviled. American entertainer James Dignitary got one of these vehicles and needed to customize it. He taught George Barris, a man who was known for his film Vehicle Sorcery, to redo the vehicle. At the point when individual entertainer Alec Guinness saw the car, he told Senior member, On the off chance that you get in that vehicle, you will be discovered dead in it around this time one week from now.

Amazingly, it was valid. Moreover, it wasn't simply a Senior member who discovered his consummation through the vehicle. Its following three proprietors all wound up harmed, once in a while, lethally, after buying the car when the tires were moved over to an alternate vehicle. The two of them extinguished simultaneously, coming about in one more accident.

2. Ötzi the Iceman - Researchers were excited by the disclosure of Otzi The Iceman. He was found on September nineteenth, 1991, when German vacationers Helma and Ariga Simon cleared off in an unexpected direction in the Alps on the Austrian Italian fringe.

They had, in one way or another, unearthed the preserved survives from Ötzi, who'd been there for a considerable number of years. Awful climate conditions implied that it took four days to uncover Otzi from the ice finally, and a few people feel that his body, done being very still, is the thing that began the revile.

Researchers Rainer Hene was the first to confront the revile. He'd been the one to eliminate Otzi's body. Moreover, when he was en route to give a discourse about the Iceman, he was engaged in a fatal mishap that guaranteed his life. The fundamental analyst, Kurt Fritze, died in a torrential slide despite being an accomplished guide. At last, Helmut, who found Otzi disappeared in the Alps. It ended up that he'd fallen more than 300 feet, yet nobody was sure how.

3. The Mirror of Myrtle's manor - Myrtle's estate is a tremendous house in Louisiana that is believed to be one of the most spooky spots in the States. There's a weird relic inside known as the Spooky Mirror. Its story originates from the individuals who lived inside the house during its prime long periods of activity. Numerous enslaved people dealt with the estate and endured shocking treatment. They were monitored by Sarah Woodruff, the frightful proprietor of the house, when she, in the long run, died. The legend says that her Soul got caught inside this mirror as discipline for her terrible deeds.

If guests take photographs of the mirror, they can supposedly observe through to the opposite side, where the Soul's hands are squeezed, facing it, trying to get out. On the off chance that you look sufficiently close, some state you may even observe the entire body. Okay, challenge investigation?

4. Basano Vase - If you get talented a jar as a wedding present, perhaps consider hiding it securely, so you don't succumb to a similar revile that this family did.

The Basano Container was cut from silver in the fifteenth century, and Fables says he was talented to an Italian lady as a wedding present. She was found grasping the jar in a ton of agony on her wedding night. As she blurred away, she vowed to look for her vengeance. Accidentally, the pot was gone on through different relatives who all shockingly died under secretive conditions. Inevitably, after somebody connected the container to these mysterious ailments, it was shrouded away for quite a long time.

Some state it was covered on the holy ground by a minister, while others state that it essentially vanished, possibly to be rediscovered in 1988 when it was found. There was a note inside that read Be careful. This jar brings demise. Ignoring this as meager more than fiction, the container was purchased, and the following three proprietors all tumbled to a similar destiny.

5. The reviled rocks of Uluru - Not exclusively is it thought to be a revile to take the stones from Uluru, yet it's very unlawful.

Numerous sightseers have taken a small bunch of the sharp rocks from the sacrosanct milestone in Australia, yet hundreds have likewise returned them, asserting the stones have prompted only misfortune. Public Park officers state they got, at any rate, one bundle a day with expressions of remorse and subtleties of ailments, bombed relationships, and deadly mishaps from the stones. Native otherworldliness is as yet noticeable in the region, and leaving the rocks in their regular habitat appears to be a simple method to keep the spirits settled.

Leon, another Native clan that lives in the region of the stone, has advanced for guests to leave all that they find precisely where it has a place, and we're beginning to get why.

6. Annabella, the doll - There are two Annabelle dolls you may have known about. However, the primary highlight in a film of a similar name is a porcelain doll that unleashes ruin and frightens everybody around her. Luckily, she's just an anecdotal character. Lamentably, the other Annabell doll out there is 100% genuine.

The primary contrast about this, Anabella, is that she's a raggedy ann doll, which makes her look significantly less unpleasant and much more soothing than her porcelain sister. In any case, that is the place the amenities end. The genuine doll was purchased from a used store and given to a young lady named Donna, who was concentrating on turning into a medical attendant at the time. Throughout the long term, Annabelle seemed to move around Donna's home, first from the sofa to the floor but then between various rooms.

Things started to get frightening when the doll began to go out. The straw that broke the camel's back came when Donna returned home one day to discover Annabel with exacting blood on her hands. Donna took the doll to a medium, saying that a little youngster's Soul was caught within it.

7. The revile burial chamber of Tutankhamun - Prehistorian Howard Carter and his support, Master Carnarvon, first found the internment office of this overlooked kid ruler in Egypt in 1923. It was covered up in the Valley of the Lords and, in contrast to different burial places, hadn't been assaulted by looters.

This was clear because the burial chamber was loaded with treasure. But instead of remaining quiet about their disclosure, the pair went to press and immediately gathered a ton of consideration. And afterward, everything began to turn out badly. First, Ruler Carnarvon got chomped by a mosquito and instantly died. Some said this was brought about by the scourge of the mummy, whose spot of rest had been disturbed. Carnarvon's pet immediately died a short time later, alongside the radiologist who probably X-beam the mummy.

Next, a wealthy American vacationer who'd visited the burial chamber tumbled to a similar destiny alongside an individual from Carter's unearthing group when a show of the discoveries was because of happening at Oxford College in Britain. The group was recognizably stressed that the clear revile would come and strike them also. Fortunately, it appears to have been broken, and nobody else has been lethally harmed since.

8. The Dybbuk box - If somebody advises you not to open something, you will need to investigate considerably more, correct? In any event, that was what occurred with the puzzling Dybbuk Box. The proprietor had gotten the crate from her grandma, a Holocaust survivor who had consistently cautioned all of her to it shut. She asserted that it was held inside a devil called a Dybbuk, which had been inadvertently gathered and detained inside the container.

In the past, the crate was available to be purchased, and the new proprietor disregarded the notice and opened up the case. Anyway, after messing with the box, his home was bafflingly stripped. However, nothing was taken. He gave a chance to his mom, who included a stroke, within five minutes of getting it. The entirety of the following individuals to possess the case asserted it had a quality of misery and perniciousness encompassing it.

9. Maori fighter Masks - Some of these condemnations existed years back and are a distant memory now. However, the Maori champion veils are things that are still an idea to be revealed right up to the present time. The Maori are the indigenous individuals of New Zealand who intensely accepted the profound world and its condemnations. Even though the practices aren't as essential in the 21st century, the way of life still broadly knows about one ordinary reviled object. Inside the way of life are their hero veils made before fights. The covers were thought to hold the Soul of any man who died during the battle.

Even though the veil would be okay for many people to wear, it was considered hazardous for pregnant or discharged ladies to go close to it. The thinking behind this is that pregnancy was considered a no-no or no-no in the way of life, as are the relics. Therefore, if the two are joined, it's the idea that a revile could be conjured. There's no confirmation, yet historical centers that show the covers frequently set up signs clarifying that pregnant ladies should remain away in the event of some unforeseen issue.

10. Busby's Chair - Busby's seat hangs high up on the roof to keep anybody from ever sitting on it again.

Legend has it that the seat had a place with Thomas Busby, who didn't care for anybody sitting in his home when he got into contention with a man who alienated him by sitting in his seat. Thomas chose to dispose of him unequivocally. At the point when Busby died before long, he reviled the chair, announcing that demise would come to any individual who sat in it. Through the mid-1970s, the chair, which remained in Busby's drinking foundation, appeared to guarantee various casualties, from the housekeeper to irregular spectators who had chosen to take the risk.

After all these events, the chair was hung to spare people's lives.

CHAPTER THIRTEEN

WHEN KING SOLOMON MET THE SEVEN SISTERS OF HELL

In the Confirmation of Solomon, we truly observe our saint Solomon put under a magnifying glass as he goes head to head against not one, not two, but rather seven spirits simultaneously, all of which have a comment.

Unlike his experiences with the Devil Asmodeus and the breeze evil spirit Tephras, these seven elements are more likened to talking. They don't seem to compromise Solomon, at any rate, not straightforwardly.

It isn't the first run-through Solomon goes head to head against spirits of the female influence. We can see him take on the demoness Onoskelis, and he has the option to oppose her charms as though they were everyday teases. Be that as it may, these seven female spirits who appear to him in this piece of the story are not here to be a tease. Instead, they carry their premonition feeling of risk while never explicitly alluded to as devils.

They do believe themselves to be goddesses. Solomon lets us know from the very get-go that there came seven spirits, females bound and woven together, reasonable in appearance. Solomon saw them, questioned them, and stated, who, right? Be that as it may, in unanimous agreement, they said with one voice; we are the 33 components of the infinite leader of the dimness.

Immediately, there is a ton to dismember here. I'll make a valiant effort to be as exhaustive as possible under the circumstances; we can tell there are seven female spirits bound and woven together. What's more, by this, a few researchers have decided to be seven sisters. Given the amount of a cozy relationship, these devils and spirits need stars and heavenly bodies in this story; it's been hypothesized that these seven sisters are the Pleiades. That which is an open star bunch in the northwest celestial body of Taurus, which additionally has the name Seven Sisters.

God refers to the Pleiades in the Book of Work, where he scolds Employment by asking him, Would you be able to tie the chains of Pleiades? Whether God is alluding to the group of stars or the seven sisters included in the Confirmation of Solomon isn't known. Besides, we comprehend from Jewish and Babylonian fables that detestable spirits are frequently bound in Sevens, so it bodes well that these substances appear to Solomon in a gathering of seven.

Another thought is that the sisters here speak to the seven different planets in our nearby planetary group. They, at that point, start to present themselves individually.

The first is named Duplicity. The second is called difficulty. The third is named Klothod, which means fight. The fourth is named envy. The fifth is named Force.

The 6th is named Error, and the seventh proclaims that she is the to top it all off, yet doesn't uncover her name. She likewise expresses all stars are in paradise, seven stars humble in Sheen and all together. Furthermore, we are called, in a manner of speaking, goddesses. We changed our place together and lived here and there in Lidya, now and then in Olympus, some of the time on an extraordinary mountain.

Here we discover that every single one of the seven sisters appears to speak to something much the same as the seven fatal sins, however not precisely. They say to something of man's most exceedingly terrible ascribes, including his capacity to deceive the struggle he may cause or harm his impact on the climate through his fights and wars, the torment, his envy causes the Force which makes him frantic and the Mistake which he submits when he sins.

These sisters represent the entirety of our most exceedingly awful characteristics; clearly, they are not such creatures who the equitable individual would decide to connect with. Moreover, we get a brief look at the presumption that they proclaim that they have stars in paradise, or once more, a similar ramification that different devils have made in that they accept they have a spot in heaven or had begun there. They even allude to themselves as goddesses, putting themselves on a similar level to God.

On the off chance that we've taken in anything from Lucifer, we realize that such aspirations are not met with outcomes. They likewise reveal to Solomon that they are very portable spirits and that they persuade around now and then to be found in Lidya and some of the time in Olympus; again, we see the content creators straightforwardly reference components of Greek folklore. What's more, it may be that these animals are the relatives of the Titan Chartbook. Might you trust it called the Pleiades, which, as referenced prior, is the thing that the group of stars in the Taurus heavenly body is named after?

Curiously, if we take a gander at one of the stories from folklore, the sisters execute themselves in the wake of learning the destiny of their dad Chartbook. A short time later, Zeus has compassion for them and reveres them as stars. By this, it is no big surprise they allude to themselves as goddesses being the relatives of Map book. It is additionally no big surprise why they imply to Olympus just like their home. Their reality under this thought of them being goddesses of any nature isn't viable with Solomon's God. Thus you may state that they're in for a reality check if they believe they will pull off such an apostasy.

We've seen Solomon's god hand out disciplines for far less. Solomon starts to scrutinize its Soul, and they reveal to him which heavenly attendant it is they dread the most and which holy messenger it is that has the most control over them. We get a touch of understanding into every one of these sisters as they separately discuss Solomon; Duplicity lets him know I delude and weave catches to a great extent. I mind and energize blasphemies. This is obvious in that Double-dealing lays snares for devotees and looks to board them off the proper way by either fooling them into transgression or engaging their allurements.

Conflict reveals to him that I bring lumbers, stones, sheds, and my weapons on the spot. Furthermore, we can tell from this that conflict utilizes the most challenging things on earth, such as stones and lumbers, to illustrate the problematic situations that devotees may end up giving her. She pronounces that these hot properties are her weapons, and she's not short of conveying them to humanity.

Klotho, or fight, discloses to Solomon that I caused the polite to dissipate and fall foul of the other. What's more, usually, we discover that she impels inside humankind the need to battle, paying little mind to how gentle their disposition can be.

The desire is one more who is clear as crystal; as she discloses to Solomon, I cause men to overlook their restraint and control; I pass them and split them into parties, for struggle follows me inseparably. I read the spouse from the sharer of his bed and youngsters from guardians and siblings from sisters. She looks here to show Solomon that as desire, she can drive a wedge between any relationship. Because of her interfering conflict, she thinks it's simpler to strike as she causes the people to languish over their envy.

Force pronounces that by the power I raise dictators and destroy lords to all revolutionaries I outfit power. Again she is pretty simple to peruse, given the idea of what Force is. She's ready to flaunt the individuals who might make her offering as despots, but on the other hand, is quick to destroy lords, inferring that she needs oppression and needs rulers who will do awful in her name. She's also quick to outfit power inside agitators, potentially those who defy God and try to destroy others for their confidence.

Just once we arrive at Mistake second with Solomon, things get genuinely intriguing, for Error truly gives Solomon something to consider. She discloses to him I will make thee fail as I had before made thee to Error, at the point when I caused thee to kill thy sibling. I will lead you into Error to get into graves and instruct them that burrow and I lead evil spirits from all devotion and numerous other insidious characteristics are mine. Here we see Mistake assumes liability for the passing of Solomon's sibling at the Niger, who Solomon had executed in a question for rulership in the Good's Book of Rulers.

It positions Error in a place of control over Solomon, and it is inferred that she had just previously controlled him, much as she controls each man to commit past errors. It would likewise suggest that Solomon wasn't right to slaughter his sibling and that maybe it mixed up his sibling's aims to take the seat for himself. Here, Error planted the seed of uncertainty in Solomon's psyche, and she might be the leading Soul of the seven sisters who get him to re-think himself. She reveals to him that she will lead him to make the Error again and likewise do this to numerous other men, for that is her obligation.

The seventh Soul is a tricky and anonymous one who proclaims herself the most exceedingly terrible. Additionally has her turn and says, I am the most noticeably awful, and I exacerbate the off than thou wast because I will force the obligations of Artemus. Yet, the grasshopper will liberate me, for by implies thereof is it destined that thou shalt accomplish my craving. If one were shrewd, he would not turn his means towards me. Here we see the seventh Soul undermined Solomon, that she will aggravate him off than what he was previously and that she will force the obligations of Artemus while this isn't clarified in the content.

It is conceivable that the seventh Soul alludes to the folklore whereby Artemus transformed men into creatures as she does with the Tracker Actaeon, who unearths her washing. Artemus transforms this guiltless tracker into a stag and sets Actaeon's canines upon him in retribution. The seventh Soul may mean this from a symbolic perspective, and that she transforms men into creatures, or that she twists their psyches until they show up more monster than human and along these lines more inclined to viciousness and hostility.

This is only one unverified thought. The second piece of her statement is of more interest to us. Furthermore, as she says, the grasshopper will liberate her, for it is destined that Solomon will accomplish her craving without giving an excessive amount of away.

We see Solomon giving up five grasshoppers to strange divine beings toward the finish of the confirmation as he betrays God with the end goal of lying down with an agnostic lady. It may be the case that this function is foreshadowed here by the seventh Soul, who at last gets her way by Solomon's penance as he wanders off the author's way since he utilizes beetles to do this. The insects, in actuality, are what achieve her triumph. Solomon doesn't have the foggiest idea about this yet.

She likewise cautions that Wiseman would do whatever it takes not to play with her, for they will meet terrible destinies on the off chance they do. Solomon's intelligence demonstrates how imposing the Seventh Soul is, for not even he can overcome her at long last. Yet, similar to what I stated, Solomon doesn't know about her capacity at a reasonable time in the story; you may even say he thinks little of her, given that he continues to take them all with the ring and powers them to burrow the establishments of the sanctuary.

He lets us know, "So I, Solomon, haven't heard and pondered, fixed them with my ring, and since they were so extensive, I paid them to burrow the establishments of the Sanctuary of God for its length was 250 cubits, and I paid them to be enterprising. What's more, with one mumble of joint dissent, they started to play out the undertakings delighted in." The Greek impact radiates unequivocally in this piece of the story; accordingly, we are blessed to receive some pretty convincing devils that don't come around in the Good Book.

It is the thing that confirmation of Solomon is such fun. Clever read, for it doesn't simply give us the symbolic evil presences and theoretical thoughts, however instead, the natural appearances of some appallingly fearsome and inventive characters that test Solomon, yet provide us with a feeling of how immense the scene of damnation could be and that such creatures are prowling there.

CHAPTER FOURTEEN

THE SATANIC POSSESSION OF THE NUNS OF LOUDON

Loudun, France, 1632; it's late around evening time when out of nowhere, Jeanee arose from a profound rest to discover a man remaining over her tangle; the secretive outsider sobbed, imploring her to ask with him bobbling in dread; she pardoned herself and fled, getting another religious recluse who saw only for the remainder of the night, the two of them were upset by puzzling murmurs.

Throughout the following few days, Jeanee started seeing the ghost during the daytime. In some cases, he implored her to supplicate. At times he murmured suggestive things to her. Jeanee's hair stands on end. It seemed like her very bones tingled. Before long, many nuns in the Ursuline Religious community of Loudon started encountering comparable side effects. Blood hustled through their veins, and their hearts beat. They daydreamed. Voices encourage them to do evil, regardless of how much compensation is for self-flogging. The nuns performed. The side effects endured.

Their questioner thought evil spirits controlled them. He started holding expulsion, sprinkling the nuns with sacred water, and asking over them. The nuns shouted out and naked like felines. They showed up and twisted their bodies into sexual positions.

By the authority of God, the cleric requested to realize who might revile the ladies of Christ. The eyes of one of the nuns strolled once more into her head in a deep voice exuded from her mouth. Metropolitan Grandier addressed the evil spirit. Father Metropolitan Grandier, the ministry had been sold out by one of their own.

In 1617, Metropolitan Grandier was selected as the ward cleric of the Congregation of Holy person Pierre Du Marche in the unassuming community of Loudon. He made a mix when he showed up at his post. He was attractive, affluent, and accomplished. Throughout the following hardly any years, Grandier earned significant notoriety.

Notwithstanding the way that clerics should be abstinent. He had mystery undertakings with a few ladies of the town. Intelligent and sharp, Grandier was acceptable at condemning residents who couldn't help contradicting him. Some felt he was thoughtful to Huguenots Protestant Christians who accepted that essential, dedicated confidence was preferable in strict life to the Roman Catholics' sumptuous functions. There had been a continuous force battle between the authoritarian organizations for quite a while, and Grandier ended up in its center. His sexual capers and political convictions made him many adversaries and fanned the fire. Then, in 1626 close to Loudon, the Ursuline cloister was set up.

The community immediately became a famous spot to send respectable little girls who couldn't be offered because of the absence of cash for an endowment or other reasons. One of only a few delights of the Austaire lives of the Ursuline nuns was tattling about residents, the most mainstream theme being Father Grandier. After the main Prioress died in 1627, another predominant was designated Jeanne des Anges. She had been shipped off the religious community since her hunchback, and ugly appearance made her marriage possibilities poor. Aggressive Jeanne controlled in lied her way into being selected as Mother Unrivaled. Even though the ladies ran the religious shelter, they admitted to a male cleric. Jeanne was fixated on Grandier and requested that he be the community's cleric. He declined the honor in different records Grandier needed the position, yet because of his conduct, he wasn't viewed as an appropriate inquisitor for unadulterated youthful ladies of Christ.

In any case, Father Mignon, who had real notoriety, was chosen to be the questioner for the nuns of Ursaline.

In 1630, some of Grandier's faultfinders figured out how to bring charges against him for unethical behavior. An adversary, the diocesan of Poitiers, saw him as liable. Notwithstanding, because of his associations with high political figures, Grandier was reestablished to total administrative obligations within the year. Not long, the Loudon district was struck by a typhus plague, and the religious circle in different territories self-isolated to restrict introduction to affliction; At the same time, the epidemic primarily died down after around a half year, tension, suspicion, and other psychological wellness issues were wild among the residents. At this point, Jeanne had been Prioress for about five years. She was responsible for seventeen nuns with an average age of 25.

For quite a while, Jeanne had stewed over the way Father Grandier wasn't the inquisitor for the religious shelter. She worked herself into visualizations or lied and guaranteed she was encountering mind flights. Genuine or not, she admitted to Father Minyong about dreams of Grandier torturing her.

Father, Minyong, and his right hand, father Weave, were not fanatics of Grandier. They speedily made this odd circumstance advantageous for them. Afterward, a portion of the nuns was to guarantee that the father, Minyong, hassled and fooled him into being controlled. It's conceivable that the Priest of Portier planned with Father Minyong to get the nuns to guarantee that Father Grandier had charmed them. Lost to history, side effects spread all through the nuns, and soon the more significant part of the convent was beset with ownership. The nuns experienced everything from fits to beatings to Undetectable Phantom and Hives.

Inquisitively, a portion of the nuns appeared to communicate in unknown dialects out of nowhere or showed superhuman quality and a large group of other insane side effects. Fa- the Minyong held expulsions at the religious community when implored over or sprinkled with sacred water. The nuns responded, turning their bodies into odd shapes, articulating lewdnesses and deep voices, and roughly propositioning the ministers in realistic sexual terms. When addressed, a portion of the nuns named the Devils, who had assumed control over their bodies. Others, particularly Jannae, asserted that Grandier had allured them and that he was a performer rehearsing the dim expressions. From the start, Garnier is wary and ignores the nun's claims it was a silly error. The Black magic Demonstration of 1604 required capital endless supply of divination, Black magic, and ruthless agreement. The allegations of black magic continued, and Grandier started to pay attention to the issue.

And mount a guard. He composed the diocese supervisor of Bordeaux, who sent his doctor to analyze the nuns. The specialist found no proof of true belonging in the Spring of 1633. The diocese supervisor requested the expulsion stopped and the cloister sequestered.

The issue subsided for a while. Yet, later in the year, the craziness returned. Cardinal Richelieu, who held influence in the Catholic Church and as Lord Louis, the thirteenth boss pastor, got included in the legislature's interest. Already, Richelieu and Grandier had conflicted over Huguenot's issues. In November 1633, Richelieu named a political cohort of his Jean De Lauberdemont as a head of a commission to research if Grandier was a witch. As a precautionary measure, Grandier was captured and detained in the Algiers mansion so he could not escape the territory. The ministers continued expulsions, yet with a curve. Rather than being held at the abbey, the removals started being held openly. Notwithstanding father Minyong and Father Barres, two different clerics who spent significant time in displacement, Father Tranquile and Father Lactans joined the procedures of the 7000 onlookers who came to see the nuns. Seeing the sexual carrying on of the nuns turned general sentiment against Grandier, and vast numbers of the residents changed from Protestant to Catholicism because of the public executions. In the interim, the commission addressed Grandier, including further allegations they constrained him to sign proclamations and refusals, which Lubardemont then took to the illustrious court in Paris. The Commission additionally blocked letters and petitions from Grandier allies in May of 1634 Lubardemont got back to Loudon with a declaration of the board broadening his forces and denying parliament and all different adjudicators from meddling in the issue, just as disallowing all gatherings worried from engaging under punishment of a fine.

A few Grandier allies decided to escape France because they dread the specialists censuring them as embellishing witches. During the preliminary, a supposed settlement made between Grandier and the villain was exposed. The settlement, which affirmed Grandier as insidious deception, was supposed to be taken from Lucifer's bureau of shrewd arrangements by one of the torturing evil spirits. The arrangement, purportedly composed in reverse by Grandier in Latin and marked in blood outland, Grandier his obligation to the villain and the advantages he would get consequently. Cosigners were Satan, Lucifer, Beelzebub, Elimi, Leviathan, and Astaroth, and it was authorized by Mark and Sign of the Central Fiend and My Rulers, the Sovereigns of Hellfire.

A few nuns, including Jeanne des Anges, started abjuring their declarations of ownership, broadcasting Grandier's honesty. She even showed up in court with a noose around her neck, taking steps to hang herself if they didn't let her retract her earlier lies. Eventually, 72 observers swore proof against Grandier doing without ordinary court strategies.

The illustrious commission immediately passed the sentence on August eighteenth, 1634. Metropolitan Grandier was seen as blameworthy of divination in setting evil spells to scrub the ownership of the Ursuline nuns. His discipline was to be copied alive at stake. Before his execution, Grandier was exposed to different torments, including the boot, to compel him to name his accessories; however, they broke two legs. Grandier, wouldn't give names.

He was sorry for his past prurient ways; however, he unflinchingly kept up his honesty about black magic and any agreements with the fiend. Frequently the sentenced were permitted to offer a last expression to the group and were humanely choked before being scorched at stake. Notwithstanding, Grandier was not allowed this little kindness. When he was on the framework, the ministers deluged him with holy water, keeping him from talking. Likewise, Father Lactance lit the memorial service fire before the killer could choke Grandier, making him scorched alive. However, Grandier had the final word as he battled against the flares. Grandier supposedly told from their bolted horns that he would see God in 30 days, and it was right. Father Lactance kicked the bucket within a month. Indeed, Grandier's passing appeared to release a revile upon a few people engaged with the preliminary inside five years, Father Quiet, one of the preliminary adjudicators, Louis Chauvet, and Dr. Monarry, a fake doctor, fell into a daze and kicked the bucket crazy. Father Barre, in the end, wound up being exiled from the congregation for contriving to blame a cleric for assault on the Special stepped area. Not long after Grandier's passing, Father Jean Joseph Seweryn came to London to perform expulsions. Jeanne De Anges had flip-slumped to, and fro between being had and guaranteeing that she lied father, endeavored an eviction for her, and purportedly got controlled by Jeanne's demons. Frequently, he went into a moderate decrease, in the end getting incapable of eating, dressing, walking, perusing, or composing. He attempted to end it all. However, he was taken in by the Jesuit school at Santa Claus and was gradually breastfed back to well-being.

Nonetheless, Jeanne De Anges recuperated from her disease. She wound up voyaging to France, showing the curious physical signs from God that were verification of her expulsion and extraordinary recuperating: the name of Jesus, Mary, and Francois de Deals inexplicably and permanently scratched on her left hand. The displacements proceeded until 1637, 3 years after Grandier's passing. They had turned into a very vacation destination; two times per day aside from Sundays, the burdened nuns were exorcized for the titillation of the groups.

At last, Cardinal Richelieu cut off monetary help, and the shows finished.

CHAPTER FIFTEEN

NECROMANCY: THE ART OF SUMMOUNING THE DEAD

We generally observe enchantment through a wide range of fiction and works of imagination.More often than not, it furnishes us with a significant plot gadget; it permits us to lower ourselves in a world that feels natural yet special and fantastical in works of imagination and fiction.

It's expected to see sorcery portrayed as light, dim, great, and cruel. There are worthy practices and, afterward, those that are a no-no. Necromancy, a training that many order as dark wizardry or dull black magic, is a school of sorcery that ought not to be polished. However, that wasn't generally the situation. Furthermore, we'll investigate a portion of the beginnings of Necromancy, how it advanced, and what models we have today. Before we go any further, we first need to characterize Necromancy.

The term itself alludes to an act of witchcraft that revolves around speaking with the dead. This can include calling the soul or, in any event, raising their whole body as the soul would not be viewed as a component of our reality. Consequently, they accepted they would approach the past, present, and future.

Hustling them genuinely is something we see from the individuals who wish to bring a friend or family member back from their dead, or sometimes they're even utilized as a weapon to make the offering of their lord.

The word itself started from the Latin Necromantia, which was taken from the Greek Necromantia, which implied divination by the methods for a dead body. This brings us to the absolute most punctual records of Necromancy, which occurred in Greece and Rome, alongside Egypt and Babylonia.

These practices are frequently contrasted with shamanism, and there was no disgrace or idea of bad behavior regarding sorcery. This is something that went to a lot later.

There was a training in antiquated Greece called Negia or Nekia, a ceremony or a custom where the dead would be called upon to respond to inquiries regarding what was to come. Probably the most punctual model of this specific sort of sorcery originates from Homer's Odyssey, where we see the incredible alchemist, Sarsie, who is fit for the explanation and communing with the dead.

Sarsie, at that point, shows vast numbers of these spells to Odysseus, the story's legend. She then encourages him to venture out to the hidden world and play out a nekia to assemble the data required for him to get back securely. In Book 11 of Homer's Odyssey, Odysseus was told to raise the soul of the visually impaired prophet Tiresias, and this specific ceremony is depicted in some detail. He should initially light a fire in the corner of the night and afterward penance creatures whose blood would be given to the shades or spirits to drink.

While doing this, he would recount the chants given to him by Sarsie. Odysseus experiences a few spirits before observing the prophet, the most eminent of these being his mom, what his identity was stunned to see since he accepted that she was as yet alive. When Tirasias finally shows up, he drinks the blood. He gives Odysseus the data expected to make it home first, encouraging him not to eat the cows of Apollo to abstain from acquiring his fierceness. He also discloses that he will get back alone with none of his group.

We can see from this specific model that Necromancy wasn't viewed as a malicious type of sorcery, a remarkable inverse. Various Greek and Roman artists who might remember these ceremonies for their accounts would utilize this magic.

It was a typical saying for Greek and Roman saints to play out a therapy, a physical excursion to the hidden world that included playing out an assignment or a mission, and much of the time, fellowship with the dead. Those resurrected in the dead were alluded to as warlocks, and it appeared when it came to bringing in one's body, they would essentially zero in on the individuals who had passed on as of late inside a year or two. Ceremonies of sorcery would, in general, change.

As we found in Homer's Odyssey. They can be very twisted, including creature penance and, now and again, even mutilation and utilization of the dead. Different occasions include practices, for example, wearing the dress of the perished and devouring food, for example, darkened bread and unfermented grape juice, which was thought to represent the rot and inertia of death. It was genuinely regular practice to see antiquities, for example, charms and wands, utilized close by these spells. So when did sorcery become this dark heart, this school of magic that was viewed as unsuitable or untouchable?

Most sources point towards the period of archaic Europe when the congregation truly started to get serious about sorcery and black magic. Witchcraft was one of those practices to be criticized as unsafe.

The congregation marked the demonstration of Necromancy as Evil, a demonstration of black magic with the expectation of doing hurt.

Necromancy would be compared to raising devils who covered up under the pretense of spirits.

The congregation accepted that revival itself was a demonstration that must be performed with the help of God. Also, strikingly enough, various pastorates played out specific degrees of Necromancy.

These experts were quite often profoundly prepared and taught in soothsaying, demonology, and expulsion, joined in the Christian, Jewish and Arabic lessons that revolved around sorcery; specialists of Necromancy or Necromancers sketched out three things they accept could be accomplished through the training, information, dream and the capacity to control the desire of others. These three things can be found in a positive and negative light. It just comes down to where you stand. On one side, the congregation who accept those outsides would utilize Necromancy to hurt others and advantage themselves.

Furthermore, the individuals not related to the congregation considered it an endeavor to control and restrict this type of witchcraft so it would just profit the community.

Whether you accept these ceremonies and this specific school of enchantment is genuine is totally up to you. My position on Necromancy is equivalent to my work on the extraordinary and a wide range of fantasies and legends. I don't have faith in these accounts, yet I accept they made and propelled fascinating thoughts and models that we utilized and still use today in narrating.

We would now be able to investigate some more present-day models and how the original sorcerer is utilized today.

One that a significant number of us would have gone over lately is Tolkien's character, Sarum, the dull master who passed by numerous titles. One of these is the Necromancers. The individuals who have viewed the films and possibly read a portion of the books may ask why he was given this title since raising the dead isn't something we find in any motion pictures. Notwithstanding, throughout the entire existence of Center Earth, a progression of volumes gathered by Tolkien's child from the entirety of his dad's compositions in Volume 10 is more coauthoring.

We see a statement that reveals that he is undoubtedly equipped for fellowship with the dead, subjugating them and saddling their insight. If we investigate the Mortal Kombat establishment, we have Shang Tsung and Quan Shi, who accept parts of warlocks and alchemists who fiddle with the craft of Necromancy.

The two cases center around raising the dead to shape armed forces for their lord and eventually make their offering.

Raising a multitude of the undead is sincerely something that we see from most sorcerers.

What's more, in Harry Potter, we have Ruler Voldemort. This wizard rehearsed sorcery, raising a whole multitude of skeletons and zombies during the principal wizarding war, generally comprised of the individuals who had just been killed. We also observe something like this with the white walkers and the late evening ruler of Round of Seats, who can raise the dead by lifting his arms. These models have insidious expectations and are the antagonists of the regarded stories.

However, as we've just observed, sorcery wasn't constantly viewed as dull craftsmanship, and not all warlocks are portrayed as underhanded.

We've just examined the account of Odysseus, the saint of Homer's Iliad and The Odyssey. On the off chance that we investigate the Wonder Universe and Black Panther and explicitly T'Chala, Sister Suri can vivify the dead, and she's no lowlife. We additionally have the fairly fascinating case of Dr. Frankenstein, who many consider a sorcerer, who positively didn't have a detestable aim. I do discover the instance of Dr. Frankenstein to be very weird because you can contend that he raised the dead, and in this way, he qualifies as a Necromancer.

Yet, I will generally glance at him as a man of science and his beast as a creation.

So I surmise we need to solicit ourselves, other than the impact of the congregation during the middle age, for what reason are endless sorcerers in fiction evil? It comes down to how they make great lowlifes when you rout the reprobate armed force; you anticipate that the fight or the war should be finished. Be that as it may, sorcerers can call new militaries from the corpses.

Given this sentiment of misery, they additionally have a degree of information acquired through communing with the dead that makes them something other than an imposing foe.

There is additionally this no-no regarding the wrecking of the dead and simply leaving them to find happiness in the hereafter. Consequently, raising the dead can be viewed as bold and even evil now and again. There are a few parts of Necromancy that we don't generally need to see through a perspective of sick purpose, for example, speaking with the dead.

In conclusion, how you decide to see Necromancy is eventually your decision.

CHAPTER SIXTEEN

MARIE LAVEAU: VOODOO QUEEN

There's something to be said about the city of New Orleans, the city that so significantly catches both the old world and the new and its endless nightlife, it is prestigious cooking, and the festivals of the different African, French, and American cultures.

In reality, it seems like such a spot where wizardry could occur. It would be here in the Huge Simple. This carries me to one of New Orleans' most remarkable occupants, Marie Laveau, the lady said to be the voodoo QUEEN despite having been dead for more than 200 years. Presently, individuals state that Marie Laveau controls the city, passing by what the legends state about her voodoo rehearses that would perform noteworthy accomplishments. In some form, they are supernatural occurrences.

We will essentially be zeroing in on Louisiana Voodoo or New Orleans voodoo, which is a result of the religion voodoo so vigorously impacted by the Christian and French culture of New Orleans, which Marie Laveau would turn into a staple of.

Even though there is a lot of data about Marie Laveau in New Orleans's legends, isolating current realities from fantasy isn't simple. We know little of her initial existence other than that she was likely conceived in 1801 to an affluent estate proprietor and his dark paramour, as specific sources state. Her dad, also called Charles Laveau, may likewise have been something of a lawmaker proceeding to turn into a city hall leader of New Orleans in 1812.

Her mom was named Marguerite and was supposed to be a voodoo professional.

We likewise realize that Laveau would wed a man named Jack Harris, a craftsman who might give her two kids.

Nonetheless, Harris would abruptly disappear in 1824, whereby Laveau would talk about his demise, professing to be a widow; however, it's similarly authentic that Harris essentially abandoned Laveau, yet that she was too prideful even to consider admitting this. She was portrayed similar to a lovely lady, tall with dull wavy hair and glowing skin. At the zenith of her reputation, tabloids would depict her as having great highlights, great highlights at that point, implying that she seemed to have the physical attributes of a white lady over a dark one.

After Harris' demise, Marie started working in the salon as a stylist. This is one of the most significant pieces of her life for us here that she would like the administration to be well-off, white, and Kreyol ladies of New Orleans, whereby they would trust in her their most closely privileged insights and want data about their spouses, sweethearts, their homes and family issues.

Many accept that this abundance of data that Laveau would get consistently is the thing that gave her political influence and is the motivation behind why she had the option to ascend through social status. Laveau might want to start a relationship with Luis Christophe de Clapham, a man from an amazing nearby family with whom she would work 15 kids in quick progression.

It would lead her to stop styling and commit her opportunity to raise her brood. She looked into her mom's voodoo rehearses and conventional African convictions; voodoo had gained notoriety for herself in Louisiana and was even prohibited at a few focuses. Many trusted it was the craft of the demon and that it was here to usurp Christianity, turning Christians and great people into a more obscure way loaded with spiritualists and sorcery.

Numerous who held this view were unaware of voodoo and conventional African convictions. They would probably decorate the training to serve their plan, referring to it as insidious, degenerate, or profane. However, this didn't stop Laveau and many of her customers from rehearsing voodoo. Laveau would take in a large portion of her art from a voodoo specialist in New Orleans who was just included and genuinely known as Dr. John, who isolates Louisiana voodoo from voodoo. Different types of the curse are the Catholic impact that individuals like Laveau injected with it.

Louisiana Voodoo would consolidate blessed water, incense, sculptures of holy people, and even Christian supplications that make it more worthy to the privileged and engage the individuals dedicated to Christianity.

Many of those convictions included otherworldly powers, as is regular in all voodoo, whereby the spirits brought can be either kind or naughty. The thought was that these spirits were associated with voodoo devotees, controlling them, giving some celestial information, or bringing great vibes. How this was accomplished through a combination of moving music, singing, and even the utilization of snakes. Laveau was even said to have won a pet snake around her neck named Zombie.

A portion of Marie's remarkable administration as a voodoo QUEEN incorporated selling GriGri sacks and a talisman from Africa, they stated, to bring fortune and shield the wearer from evil. The GriGri sacks were said to contain an assortment of fixings that were honored by voodoo QUEENs or voodoo specialists to bring the wearer a specific impact or predetermination charms, magical powders, components, and want quantum adornments, including those that could annihilate a client's adversaries, were additionally sold by Laveau.

She additionally leads profound readings, telling fortunes, offering guidance to the individuals who looked for it, and projecting spells, including fixes, charms, or even reviles at the correct cost. In any case, a few history students accept that Laveau's forces were, in reality, astute acts, and every last bit of her heavenly information about individuals' lives was procured by the account of numerous privileged insights spilled to her by her customers. Remembering she would serve multiple noticeable family units in

New Orleans, some of them liable to uncover specific touchy data.

Given how warm and sympathetic it proposed that Laveau utilize this data to differentiate her status or to manufacture the possibility that she was educated. Another record has it that Laveau would use the dark workers of rich whites to acquire data and that she would do this by imparting dread into the workers, taking steps to revile or hex them or take care of them. There is one story of Laveau's forces that would charm all of New Orleans. A rich man's child was blamed for an assault claim and was set to confront a lengthy prison sentence.

The proof against both him and the child was cursing, and it seemed to be a straightforward scenario. Frantic to guarantee his child's opportunity and now, all things considered, to accomplish it, the rich man went to Laveau for help in return for his achievement in this issue. He would offer her a house, Laveau concurred, and have the voodoo custom, where she went through a type of self-torment. She set free, ludicrously hot Guiney peppers in her mouth and held them there for quite a long time as she spoke to the spirits in voodoo.

The conviction is that the spirits have compassion for those under great affliction; thus, Laveau would utilize her agony to draw the souls out and award her what she looked for.

Upon the arrival of the consultation, Laveau snuck into the town hall and put the Guinea papers in her mouth under the seat of the adjudicator. Some accept that the energy from the profoundly upgraded peppers made the appointed authority set the well-off men without a child, similar to the arrangement the rich man inside allowed the house he had guaranteed her.

Notwithstanding, a few antiquarians question this case, expressing that if such an event did, in reality, happen, at that point, all things considered, Laveau would have known the adjudicator for her groups of friends or would, at any rate, realized something implicating about the appointed authority for which she would have used to extort him with.

She would have still utilized her voodoo-showy behavior to persuade New Orleans that she did, without a doubt, have mysterious forces. Yet, some accept that the premise of her troops was political control and terrorizing when Laveau died in 1881. She was said to have passed on with a grin all over.

Journalists at the time alluded to them not as an evil specialists of dull magic but rather as the kindest lady who carried on a moral figure who breastfed the debilitated and spread empathy among the expired and the denounced. Laveau is covered in St. Louis Graveyard in the neighborhood Appian family grave; the internments are in the vaults over the ground where the burial chamber draws in numerous guests.

Indeed, even right up 'til the present time, numerous regional chunks, including Laveau's burial chamber, stroll by guests with an X image. The thought originates from a decades-old talk that Laveau would concede wishes from past the grave if an X were set apart on her burial place. Probably, the custom goes something along the lines of denoting an X on the burial chamber, pivoting multiple times, thumping on the burial chamber, and afterward hollering out your desire. After the wish comes true, you must return and circle the X.

So It was with Laveau's Capacity and afterward left the Voodoo QUEEN a contribution. One of the primary little girls, Marie Laveau, was set to carry her mom's mantle after her passing. By certain records, she was a carbon copy of her mom; however, what she hadn't glanced at was that she needed her mom's soul. Some have said that she didn't have the glow and empathy of her mom and was more disposed to move dreadfully. One of her most prominent gifts was the capacity to satisfy the longing of any man. She would hold luxurious gatherings at Bricklayer Whiten, a structure for the assembly of blacks and whites in New Orleans, where ladies would move stripped for men, lawmakers, and high authorities. This structure, among others, would become something of a massage parlor. In any case, it was never struck by the police, who expected that if they interceded, Marie Laveau, the second, would revile them. Some would state that Marie Laveau, the second suffocated in a lake after a significant storm. Since time at that point, both Laveaus have sunk into indefinite quality.

However, Marie Laveau remains a central figure of Louisiana voodoo and New Orleans culture; gamblers even shout her name when a friend dies or before big stakes. Additionally, there have been multiple tales of sightings of the voodoo queen, even to this day. And that wraps up the story of Marie Laveau. But was she a powerful voodoo queen capable of curing and cursing and contacting spirits, or was she more of a political player using a network of spies and their cunning to enhance and embellish her abilities?

CHAPTER SEVENTEEN

SUCCUBUS: THE DEMONESS OF NIGHT

Women, you can't live with them, and you can't survive without them except if they're beautiful demoness, who in a real sense needs to empty the life from you because I figure you can be pardoned for needing to remain away. For that reason, it sounds natural. No, we are not discussing your ex.

We are examining the succubus or the succubi on the off chance you must allude to them aggregately. At the point when we think about a succubus, there are a few things that ring a bell. The more conventional among you would think about an evil spirit that lures men. These days, we consider them appealing ladies. Furthermore, somebody simply searching succubus in Google Pictures will most likely believe it's some strange interest, and it presumably is.

Some of you may even recollect that trainwreck of a film that was Jennifer's body where Megan Fox and Amanda Seyfried make out, and afterward, Megan Fox resembles, gracious, I will eat that kid you like. What's more, Amanda Seyfried compared, no, screw you when you're unusually molded thumbs, no succubus going to eat, my man. Furthermore, that is the entire story.

So I surmise we start with the definition and the inception; a succubus is a devil that appears as a lady, which drives us to the Topic of the Day. If the evil presence is a man and, at that point, transforms into a succubus, is that devilish feline fishing? Who knows? The succubus can be followed back to ancient legends in these accounts. Once the evil spirit has accepted its female structure, it then goes to its casualty in their fantasy, and the enticement cycle starts, trailed by some sexual activity which brings up the issue, what does the succubus gain from this? That is to say, laying down with men in their fantasies doesn't appear to have much potential gain.

Be that as it may, as you may expect, there is an ulterior intention behind this. There are more than a couple of speculations concerning why. One that you may be acquainted with is the possibility of the succubus taking care of the man, either eating up his tissue or taking pieces of his spirit. Various experiences with a succubus are said to leave the casualty with extreme mental weakening, causing pipedreams and passing in the most pessimistic scenario.

Some even accept that the succubus was utilized to clarify rest loss of motion. The word succubus comes from a few diverse Latin terms, one of which is succubi, which generally means mean lies underneath or underneath the bed. This likewise identifies with the succubus position corresponding to the person in question.

There are a few records of the succubus in old Jewish stories, the most celebrated model being Adam's first spouse, Lilith. She wouldn't be compliant and left the Nursery of Eden before getting one of the four evil spirit sovereigns laid down with the Archangel Samael.

Depictions given are that of a wonderful lady. However, very close, you can see distortions, for example, serpentine, similar to tails and birdlike fat, which sound remarkably like the alarms of Greek fantasy. What's more, in the later years, the narratives of these succubi were supplanted with accounts of warnings. They do so look to some extent like another animal from Greek folklore, Lamia, and thus, the lamaii and the Empousa, which were likewise rather terrible animals that could change their structure to entice men, some deciding to take care of the men they allure and others persuading youngsters to wed them, to leave them the night before the wedding.

Lamiya herself was one of Zeus' disdained sweethearts, which turned into a beast who ate up men and youngsters as vengeance for the special kids she had lost. The one Lillith was thought to get from a gathering of evil female presences in Mesopotamian folklore named Lilitu, whose identity is named after the devil Lamashtu, who might grab youngsters. At the same time, their moms breastfed, biting on their bones and drinking their blood.

She was likewise portrayed as having a somewhat upsetting appearance. So this thought of succubi as peculiar devils who take kids ranges across something beyond one culture. All through religion, the succubus is often depicted as a negative and underhanded figure; you would then anticipate that generally blessed and strict men should do whatever they can to restrict the intensity of the succubus. In any case, there are a couple of holy men who guarantee only one out of every odd succubus is malicious.

The best model we have is likely Pope Sylvester the second, and honestly, I can value the paradox of a pope guarding a sex-evil spirit. Before Pope Sylvester passed on, he admitted everything where he uncovered that a succubus had helped him move through the positions of the Catholic Church. He said that as a youngster, he ran over a lady named Mary Diana, who guaranteed him that he would dream of abundance, favorable luck, status, and information past anything humans could instruct him. There was just one condition that he stayed dedicated to just her. Thus he acknowledged he would, in the long run, become pope. Furthermore, notwithstanding his promises, his relationship with this lady proceeded stealthily. There are various records of this story.

Some accept he was so greedy for influence and cash that he called the evil spirit that appeared as a succubus at that point. What's more, that is the reason he admitted on his deathbed. In contrast, others accepted he just became hopelessly enamored and wouldn't esteem his promises over the lady he adored. In the long run, he admitted, he painted her in such a positive light. Whether this is an anecdote about a horny pope, who discovered love or a horny pope who found a succubus, I surmise we'll never know.

The Catholic Church or those related to it had some fascinating thoughts regarding respect to the succubi. In 1487, Heinrich Kramer distributed Malleus Maleficarum, otherwise called the Sledge of Witches.

The work itself, nitty-gritty writing encompassing demonology in the fifteenth century and required the demolition of witches. Black magic was illegal by the congregation, and Kramer was previously a pastor. However, he was later undermined, as the more significant part of his composed conflicted with the previously existing Catholic regulation encompassing demonology. The congregation then denounced the book for this definite explanation, just as by a few German colleges, since quite a bit of what he portrayed was either illicit or deceptive, notwithstanding the endeavors of the strict and instructive foundations.

The book worked up an enormous measure of interest, just been beat by the Holy book itself for the following 200 years. Presently, as interesting as this seems, I notice the text because Kramer does indeed examine the succubus.

As per Kramer, a succubus would gather the semen of the men she laid down with and afterward offer it to an incubus who might utilize it to impregnate a human lady. This is how he clarifies evil spirits could sire youngsters regardless of being unequipped for conventional multiplication. He then states that kids brought into the world this route were undeniably more vulnerable to devilish impact and ownership. Whether you accept any of this, I surmise, is down to you. Yet, the idea of an evil presence lady taking semen and offering it to a devil man to impregnate a human lady is pretty crazy.

Furthermore, regardless of whether we disregard the logical restrictions of Kramer's reasoning, what does the ink do then? Do they transform the semen into evil spirit semen? Then again, I would genuinely prefer not to know.

Crafted by Heinrich Kramer, some extra insanity during the witch preliminaries occurred as ladies who endeavored to lure men were blamed for being succubus in masks, and ladies who fell pregnant with only one parent present were supposed to hold the offspring of an incubus.

It sounds like an incredibly enlightened chance to exist. How we take a gander at the succubus presently has changed to a few; the word may, in any case, invoke pictures of an evil spirit, however, and after its all said and done, I'd risk a theory that the devil isn't shocking, presumably something that seems as though it has a place in a type of sex prison brimming with whips, chains, ball gags and a large group of things you wish you could unsee.

Anyway, the lesson of the story is, regardless of how strange you think individuals are, there are consistently that weirdo, a whole lot of weirdos!

The picture we have today of a succubus is generally that of a very delightful lady with great skin, great hair, and eyes you would, in a real sense, sell your spirit for. This is a glaring difference from the flaky, distorted succubi of old with their horns and bat-like wings, which are more similar to a devil than an alluring conjurer.

However, if they can change themselves from a devil to a lady, it's not preposterous to accept they can change how human they look. I'm confident it won't come as unexpected that we regularly see the succubus in the current dream.

Stephen Ruler refers to them a few times. In obscurity, Pinnacle arrangement where a succubus named Mia enables an incubus to impregnate a lady whose youngster would then turn into a scalawag, somewhat as Cramer said about how devils recreate, just as the possibility that the offspring of an incubus is bound to be influenced by evil.

Stephen Ruler likewise portrays them as sexual vampires. Furthermore, this association between the succubi and vampires bodes well, and the lines between them can be obscured due to the brutal way they act. When we consider vampires, male and female, much like the succubi, they frequently allure their casualty before they feed, as though the pursuit or the adventure of the chase is what they genuinely enjoy.

Presently, not all vampires carry on along these lines. The Strigoi is a genuine case of vampires who don't generally think about the entire enticement measure.

This thought of female vampires being succubi do likewise exist in the Nightfall arrangement; however, for the good of you and just as I, we will imagine it doesn't exist and never has ever been done.

We likewise have the Dresden Documents by Jim Butcher, which specifies Succubi and hatch, with the hero's Stepbrother being an incubus depicted as having vampire-like characteristics.

A great many people who played Universe of Warcraft would have either had or seen a warlock going around with a succubus as a pet, which is essentially a half-stripped demoness with hooves, Wings, and the whip, which, by and by, returns us to the deep-rooted saying "He who accepts the succubus as a pet is a weirdo."

It's fascinating to see the experiences behind the succubus and how these thoughts have changed over the long run. What began as essentially disturbing devils that still youngsters turned out to be increasingly more outwardly engaging and enchanting. However, if we mull over the severe impact, it's not generally a very great shock, as debasement and enticement are repeating subjects throughout most religions.

I also discover that many creators and stories remain faithful to the beginning. There will likewise be current understandings that are only horrendous for any individual who needs a decent snicker.

CHAPTER EIGHTEEN

THE GOATMAN

Somewhere down in the woodlands of Maryland, they are said to exist, an animal so unnerving and thus fierce that its name is utilized even today to alarm little youngsters and grown-ups the same. Wally is usually snickered at when referenced. Some individuals lock their vehicle entryways, especially when driving down Fletcher Town street around evening time street where is set to watch their casualties. The prior notices may have been murmured between local people as ahead of schedule as the 1960s, yet his previously referenced in the media happened during the 1970s in the neighborhood Ruler George Province paper.

The article depicts some old legends known in the region by previous eras, including himself, yet another animal known as the boa-man prowling in the forested areas. These two animals were supposed to be apparitions and spirits that frequented the forested regions and caused trouble upon those absurd enough to be discovered that night.

After fourteen days, a similar paper printed an article about a family named Edwards, who'd lost their canine named Ginger. The article proceeds to clarify after a careful inquiry by the family, the body of their canine was discovered lying on the side of Fletcher Town street, its head viciously removed. One of the principal current occurrences would become related, especially when the Edwards, his long-term old girl, and her companions professed to have seen a considerable animal close to their home the same night a canine had disappeared.

Entirely soon, a series of reports of a dark-looking creature strolling on two legs was observed along Fletcher Town Street. Would before long locate a lot bigger crowd to panic.

Notwithstanding, when The Washington Post posted an article about Beam Hayden, John Hayden, and Willie Geen, the three men answerable for discovering Ginger the canine, it would see the Goatmen become a more perceived animal among any semblance of Bigfoot and a Lochness beast.

Some have even referred to just like the Merryland Bigfoot; it might be said that the animal is both faltering to understand and then absolutely slippery. In any case, what is, or who is?

Where did it originate from, and what does it need? Accounts depict the Goatmen just like an animal that remains more than six feet tall, a half man and half goat.

He is said to be Pylos and putrid once in a while and, in particular, has a sharp screech; he has cold dark horns, unkempt and raucous hair, and substantial paw-like hands in different documents he's never observed without his trusty hatchet supported in his arms. There are numerous varieties of Maryland, which are passed down from age to age. All the more regularly or not, the brain is the Merryland boogeyman, a simple invented animal that youngsters used to prod each other with or that guardians used to terrify their kids into carrying on better.

Yet, he has a more solid presence and starting point story for other people. Some accept the goat man was a forlorn old herder who remained quiet about himself in the forested areas. Be that as it may, a couple of youngsters unearthed his group and slaughtered them one night.

When the old herder found the assemblages of his cherished goats, he went crazy with rage. The site of the goat's blood irritated him to such an extent that it influenced his physiology, handing him over to the goat man. Others accept that the herder went to sinister customs to assist them with conquering his pain. Furthermore, in an unexpected bend, the fiend transformed him into a half-breed goat, an animal never going to budge on vengeance against adolescents specifically. The story's recounting fits in with the objectives that the goat man is set to go after.

Except for canines and other family pets, adolescents across Maryland from the 1970s onwards announced a few sightings of the goat man, some of which were said to have been pursued by the animal, which hollers and screeches and makes frightful goat commotions as he runs after them. Others accept that the goat man targets darlings and that such a Fletcher town street fills in as the ideal core for this undertaking, given that the road has a notoriety for being a sweetheart's path.

Teenagers and grown-ups have utilized the encompassing zones to leave their vehicles. Given the detachment of the forested areas, it makes for the ideal space to become more acquainted with each other somewhat better without according to anybody aside from that. In specific reports, it seems, by all accounts, to be holding an enormous hatchet and jumping after clueless casualties who are getting occupied in the rearward sitting arrangement.

Reports guarantee that he crushes vehicles open with a brutal quality, breaks windows, hacks away at entryways, and even slices tires to forestall his casualty's escape. Different records guarantee that it is unmistakably more key and bait his prey out of their vehicles by making conscious sounds, urging the sweethearts to leave their cars, and examine. One of the more peculiar stories he said to be the consequence of an awful test turned out badly at the Beltsville Exploration Horticultural Center.

At long last, the speculations about this developed to be so well known among local people, and it started to get so much legitimacy that the examination place formally denied the charges. The story had become an adolescent fixation and would see numerous youngsters who were crazy go Goatman chasing in the forested areas. Nonetheless, regardless of these chasing parties, it remains a puzzle in the Maryland and Sovereign George's region's forested areas.

Many accept that the fame of the goat man was affected by the center culture of the 60s and 70s, where vehicles allowed youngsters to investigate and find their general surroundings. It was a period before the Web, and I envision the best way to encounter anything was to get out there and experience it. You couldn't simply type in Google on the off chance that you needed to see the animal, and you unquestionably couldn't have an attractive English man disclose it to you over YouTube.

You'd need to go out there and discover, and afterward, well, at that point, it may have been past the point of no return as he covered his hatchet into your head.

All joking aside, I can observe where the legends of the Goatmen got cemented in the network's regular daily existence since it advanced experience and investigation of the obscure, both geologically and maybe powerfully. Another thought said to have been brought forth was that understudies in Ruler George's Province were told to have been finding out about Greek folklore and potentially the half man half goat God skillet. It's entirely conceivable that a gathering made it of school kids who drew motivation from their course readings.

Furthermore, similar to the images of today, it inevitably picked up footing and turned into an overall wonder.

CHAPTER NINETEEN

THE AMITYVILLE HORROR: REALITY OR FICTION?

Do you accept frightening motion pictures could revile the cast or team? It appears to be exceptionally impossible if you are sound, yet what we will tell you is uncanny. Take the Ghost establishment, for example. The young lady featured in the films passed on strangely from harmful stun while making Section three when she was only 12. Her more established sister in the movie was slaughtered by her beau soon after Section two came out, and two other principal entertainers kicked the bucket either not long previously or shortly after the delivery. This could be a fortuitous event, yet it also sends shudders down the spines of those who have faith in the extraordinary.

The Exorcist revile story is far more terrible. There are a lot of film curses, yet we'll zero in on only one The Amityville Loathsomeness Certainty or Fiction. Furthermore, was there a revile?

So we should begin with what the film depended on. There was a book distributed in 1977 called The Amityville Repulsiveness by Jay Ansen, and it was about what is presently called America's Most Spooky House. This is the thing that we know from the book. The house was arranged at 112 Sea Road in Amityville, Long Island,

New York.

It's still there, actually, depicted as a 1927 Dutch provincial. It was sold for 600 5,000 dollars in 2017, significantly less than it was available, for it could get irritating as endless individuals visit the spot on a ghastliness touring journey. That is because, in nineteen 75, the mass killer Ronald DeFeo Jr. slaughtered his mother, father, two siblings, and two sisters in that house.

From the outset, he was supposed to be crazy, expressing that voices had advised him to do it. It was an odd scene for police as all the bodies were discovered face down in their beds, and it appeared there had been no battle. It's unusual because the weapon had no silencer, so nobody could sort out why individuals in the house hadn't attempted to get away or, if nothing else, move from their beds. No tranquilizers were found in the casualties, and different family members included an untouchable evil presence. Coincidentally, DeFeo has changed his story a few times throughout the long term, a little more than a year later. In 1975, George, Kathy Lutz, and their three kids moved into the house. They thought about the killings. However, the 80,000 dollars they paid for a huge old house with a pool and boat storage was out and out a deal.

Presently, it must be said that Mr. Lutz was a strict individual. On account of what he thought about the house, he asked Father Ralph J. Pecoraro to favor the spot, as per the writer of the book, who met the dad when he turned up that day on December eighteenth to select the house, he heard a voice of a man requesting he get the Hellfire out of there. Get out! Yelled the vote, and the sacred man didn't require much convincing. Afterward, in a meeting for television, the dad stated, I was additionally sprinkling holy water and heard a reasonably deep voice behind me saying, Get out.

It appeared to be so coordinated toward me that I was terrified. I felt a smack at one point on the face. He called George, mentioned what had occurred, and cautioned him not to remain on the second floor where he had heard the voice. After this poop got genuine, George woke each night at precisely three fifteen a.m., so alert that he would go for a meander. He later discovered that that is when DeFago had executed his family. The others rested; however, for reasons unknown, they all dozed on their stomachs. Mrs. Lutz began dreaming about the homicides and likewise envisioned something abnormal. She realized who had snoozed each room and what request they had been shot.

Furthermore, they found a concealed room that terrified the life out of the helpless canine. This room wasn't in the designs for the house. They considered it the Red Room. The house would load up with flies. Sporadically parts of it would turn super cold. Also, once in a while, a rotten scent would discharge from specific territories. The guardians saw evil presence faces in the chimney, green stuff emerging from keyholes. Also, if that wasn't terrible enough, their long-term old little girl made another companion that didn't exist, something portrayed as an evil presence pig with green eyes.

Entryways hammered shut on numerous events. Locks bust open on windows. Cloven hoofprints were found on the day off. Outside, a cross flipped around itself. You can watch George on YouTube discussing another event. "Before that day, I saw Cathy transform into an elderly person. That night, she lifted off the bed around three or four inches. That's right; not a lot of interest here. In any case, maybe the significant occasion was some undetectable power stepping on Cathy's chest causing injury", or the way that George saw all the individuals from his home suspending with the children stumbling, hearing voices and singing unusual tunes and the guardians toward the finish of their tie, they moved out.

The family had kept going for only 28 days. The guardians even guaranteed that the devil had followed them to another house. However, they didn't talk much to the press as they were just about at the purpose of breakdown. Incidentally, George and Cathy took lie finder tests from a portion of America's top polygraph individuals, and the two passed. A few people said getting cash from a book was a gigantic lie. However, the Lutz's lost money on the house and their things. The minister backed them up, as did paranormal examiners Ed and Lorraine Warren. Those names should sound recognizable if you've seen The Conjuring.

A quarter century later, when met by the Set of experiences Channel, George said it's straightforward to consider something a deception. I wish it were, yet it wasn't. Thus this is America. We're nothing but bad. Mass homicide cut breakdown slice evil presence story could get away from the cinema. The film turned out in 1979 called The Amityville Frightfulness, featuring James Brolin and Margot Jokester. Concerning the revile, there are seemingly insignificant details, for example, Brolin saying that while he was perusing the content, his jeans mysteriously dropped from their holder. In any case, that is not such a severe deal. Concerning Comedian, things got somewhat hazier. The one who is likewise famous for playing Lois Path in Superman experienced a progression of terrible relationships, was harmed gravely in a fender bender, failed, and wound up having a mental meltdown. She once told the press that she needed to face her evil spirits. She wasn't alluding to the house. However, it may have been a selection of words a few people look a lot into.

In twenty eighteen. She passed on of throat malignancy at age 69, which is not dubious. Alright, so shouldn't something be said about the acclaimed essayist Jay Ansen, who got the show on the road concerning how this house became public information? He kicked the bucket at age 58, not exactly a year after the film came out. He had a terrible heart, but the man first welcomed into the house to look at it as a writer and writer named Paul Hoffman.

The Lutz family thought he was a criminologist. He passed on a couple of years after the film's delivery in a fire at age 49. Concerning Ryan Reynolds, featured in 2005 revamp, he had this to state. "A ton of the team were awakening at three fifteen toward the beginning of the day, which was the point at which every one of these outrages in the house occurred. I think it was a subliminal thing. You read the content and unexpectedly pop an alert at three fifteen in the first part of the day. In any case, numerous people state the whole thing was a fabrication, and they've attempted to expose a portion of the family's cases, maybe some of the time effectively. When the family said they saw foot marks on the day off, there was no day off. It depends on who you accept, however. Indeed, even the sun remains by his attestation that the house was spooky, and he has little to pick up from lying".

James Cromarty purchased the house in 1977 and lived cheerfully there with his better half for over ten years. He told the press nothing strange ever occurred aside from individuals stopping by in light of the book and the film. So was the family lying or seeing an instance of widespread panic, or had the evil presence proceeded onward to greener fields when Cromarty and Co. showed up? We may never know, yet we'll leave you with this. Steven Kaplan, who was likewise a paranormal specialist, didn't accept the Lutz's and thus decided to compose a book about the case and to demonstrate unequivocally that it was a lie. His book was known as The Amityville Repulsiveness Connivance. It was distributed in September 1995, a quarter of a year after he kicked the bucket.

CHAPTER TWENTY

FAMOUS TERRIFYING URBAN LEGENDS

In this section, I can be of some help in presenting to you some additionally chilling stories from history. Just this time as five urban legends from around the globe. What's constantly fascinated me about most urban legends is how quickly word can spread about them and that we are ready to acknowledge them as an authentic clarification for purported extraordinary events. Sometimes we make beasts and marvels, and God realizes what else to assist us with going to some clarification to things we don't see yet, yet it is consistently the situation.

That is to say, well, things like Bigfoot and the Lochness have never been demonstrated. They haven't been disproven ever. Whether these figures I'm talking about are genuine is up to you, yet I encourage you to keep a receptive outlook on the off chance that you dare.

1. La Lorona, The Sobbing Lady - Nobody seems to know where or how this legend began; however, it's been a piece of Hispanic culture for many years.

La Llorona is depicted as being tall, slim, and, in specific renditions, favored with a characteristic marvel; with long streaming dull hair, she seems, by all accounts, to be continually wearing a white outfit, and she looks among waterways and rivulets moaning in the night as she looks for her lost kids. In certain legends, the La Llorona goes after youngsters who have unearthed her nest and will look to drag them into the profundities of a watery grave.

The most well-known understanding of this legend is that La Llorona is the soul of a destined mother who suffocated her children and now spends endlessness holding up through the waters, looking for them as the stories go. She was once known as Maria and was destined to a laborer family and would grow up to carry on with humble methods in a single variety of the story. Her magnificence grabbed the eye of numerous men over her social class. She would appreciate the consideration, frequently wearing various outfits and dresses to boost the warm gestures that she got.

In any case, Maria had two youthful children, which frightened off some possible admirers, yet made it hard for her to go to get-togethers. One morning, Maria's children were found suffocated in the waterway.

Some had said they had passed on because of her disregard one night when she was out with a man out on the town, while others proposed she had murdered them herself out of disappointment. In a more normal legend La Llorona once more, known as Maria, was a mindful lady who was merciful, enchanting, or more every one of them, a decent soul. She wedded an affluent man who seemed to cherish her, satisfying her every need and offering her the most extravagant endowments.

Yet, that would all change when Maria brought two of the man's children. What's more, much the same as that, the man she'd known would become another person; he started to have illicit relationships with other ladies, took to drinking more, and regularly disregarded her for delayed timeframes to bring up the kids without anyone else. No doubt, he no longer thought about Maria and would even proceed to remarry a lady more fit to his social standing. When he returned to Maria, which was very rarely, he did so to visit his children.

It would make Maria develop severe hatred towards her previous spouse and her youngsters. It would one day lead Maria into a frantic fury, especially after a function where her previous spouse had disregarded her and addressed his young men as though she wasn't even there trying to disdain him.

Maria tossed her kids to a nearby stream when she woke up and acknowledged what she'd done. She attempted to run close to the waterway, trying to spare them. Be that as it may, it was past the point of no return. She was set to go through day and night melancholy and the entire day grieving the loss of her children. She wouldn't eat or drink and completely dismissed herself, sitting idle, walking around the waterway in a similar white outfit, looking for her young men as though they would supernaturally turn up.

She cried unendingly as she rose, and because she refused to eat, she became balanced, so regularly she resembled a mobile skeleton. In the long run, she passed on the banks of the waterway. Some have said that her anxious soul started to show up and wander the banks of the Santa Clause Fe Stream at whatever point sunset. Her sobbing and crying for her youngsters were said to repeat through the air, and she was supposed to be viewed as a spooky ghost floating between trees along the shoreline and drifting upon the waters.

Starting there on, she was not, at this point, known as Maria yet as La Llorona, the moaning lady. While the legends change, the soul of La Llorona is said to act without benevolence. On the off chance that you end up unearthing her in one rendition of this legend, she started to execute unpredictably hauling men, ladies, and kids she experiences during her walk. Others say that she murders kids with the conviction that in doing as such, she will exchange their lives for that of the arrival of her children.

2. Also known as Manto - Otherwise known as Manto begins in Japan and is an urban legend about a spot where you'd likely feel generally defenseless on the off chance that you needed to manage a soul. That place, obviously, the bathroom. Otherwise known as Manto is supposed to be a horrendous soul who frequents public latrines. He's portrayed just like an attractive man, a characteristic the soul uses to calm casualties into a condition of interest. Notwithstanding, in different forms, he is said to be covered as the legends go; otherwise known as Manto, he frequents the last desk area in a public restroom for the most part.

The casualty is set to hear a strange profound voice that inquires as to whether they might want red bathroom tissue or blue bathroom tissue. On the off chance that the casualty picks red bathroom tissue, Otherwise known as Manto, he is set to enter the desk area with the person in question and slice separate their substance until their garments are recolored red. On the off chance that the casualty picks blue tissue, Otherwise known as Manto, chokes the loss until their face turns blue. If you're similar to me, you'd likely attempt to outfox, Otherwise known as Manto, by requesting an alternate shaded tissue.

This, in any case, was just being hauled down to the hidden world.

Indeed, it said that hands reach up from the restroom and will get you down through your defecation and down the u-twist until you arrive at Hellfire. Also, requesting a yellow bathroom tissue, Otherwise known as Manto, attempting to suffocate you in your piss, as per the legend, on the off chance that you end up in a workspace with Otherwise known as Manto. The primary response to give is that you don't need a tissue. This was Otherwise known as Manto Disregard you. However, you probably won't have anything to wipe with.

3. The Chupacabra - If you look at an animal like Bigfoot, it's difficult to see that it is named after the prints it deserts. So like Bigfoot, Chupacabra is additionally named after what it abandons. Dead creatures, however, are his favored prey, goats; Chupacabra implies Goat sucker in Spanish, and it has been accused of assaults on various animals.

However, what is even correct? It's tough to state, given that we have no photos of the animal or sound impressions. Instead, we think about the Chupacabra, onlooker accounts, and the surge of dead creatures that leave afterward. Regularly its casualties are found depleted of their blood, given Chupacabra, a Dracula hazard for transformation. The portrayal of the Chupacabra may change, yet many concur that it remains around five feet tall and has incredible legs that permit it to cover enormous separations rapidly.

It has long hooks, gleaming red eyes, and many spikes down its back. There are numerous legends about the Chupacabra's starting point, yet the most famous is that it is the result of a U.S. government hereditary qualities explored in the rainforest of Puerto Rico that turned out badly and got away. Others trust it to be an objective outsider that had gotten away from the accident spaceship. Others accept that the animal encapsulates insidiousness, God's anger, or the physical indication of Satan himself.

Sightings of the Chupacabras proceeded into the 2000s, with some, in any event, detailing carcasses of animals in Puerto Rico, Mexico, Chile, and even Florida. In any case, in each example, the Corpses have ended up being wild canines, coyotes, raccoons, or some other regular warm-blooded animal. What separates them, however, is that these creatures experienced parasitic contamination when living, making them lose their hide and take on a more skeletal, here-and-there immense-looking appearance.

So the Chupacabras of late occasions have been distinguished and give off an impression of nothing powerful extraterrestrial about them.

However, unique onlookers of the Chupacabras, thinking back to the 90s, keep up with their accounts, clarifying that the animal with dim eyes, long appendages, and spikes on its back was genuine and that specialists in the field of excusing it just because they don't get it or don't have any desire to get it.

4. The Merryland Goatman - Said to be an unbelievable half goat and half human mixture animal. The Goatman is portrayed as having the head and rump of a goat and the body of a human passing by certain legends. The goatman of Merryland is a detonating animal previously a researcher in Beltsville Horticultural Exploration Community.

The story recommends that this researcher was probing goats until one day, the examination turned out badly. Also, in some unusual bit of destiny, he was changed into the animal we presently know as the goatman, an animal currently eager for blood. He is said to be seven feet tall. He doesn't keep up the mindset of a human, yet instead is presently similar to a wild monster that goes after anybody sufficiently stupid to meander into the forested areas. In certain legends, he goes after young couples in parks cause commonly, the individuals who have driven out to a disconnected sweetheart's path type spots; there are other stories of him breaking into individuals' homes and benefiting from trained pets.

Others confirm that the goatman searches out casualties to assault them, paying little heed to their sexual orientation. In another legend, the goatman was not once a researcher but a rancher who went distraught one day after a gathering of adolescents killed his run. This made him so irritated that for some celestial error, he turned into the goatman and pledged to get revenge on any adolescent he ran over.

5. The dark-peered children - Maybe the weird- est metropolitan legend in the rundown, the dark-looked kids are accepted to be the absolute most dangerous spirits in the presence of the individuals who have experienced them.

As reputation has recently increased some fascination, it isn't easy to relate any solid or genuine proof concerning what records did and didn't occur. However, I guess that is the purpose of a legend, it might be said. The dark peered toward kids precisely that a gathering of youngsters with complex eyes and terrifying peculiarities. The sightings of these dreadful children are primarily in abandoned regions like deserted parking areas, forlorn expressways, or calm forests.

A few records have it that dark looked at kids have thumped on entryways of isolated houses and just substituted the hall until they become exhausted and leave; the kids have, as it were, with surprising persuasiveness.

Furthermore, given their age, they appear to show some pretty grown-up characteristics in how they introduce themselves.

They are said to demand being allowed in the vehicles or homes and are as often as possible spotted attempting to catch a ride on lesser voyaged streets. Indeed, sightings have been accounted for everywhere in the world. There don't appear to be any reports of what occurs if grown-up consent gives one of the kids access. Also, perhaps that is something worth being thankful for. What do they need, I wonder? Also, what do they do to the grown-ups whenever they're welcomed in? One thing is, without a doubt, on the off chance that you end up recognizing a kid deprived in no place, make sure to check their eyes before you consider attempting to support them.

About The Author

Karan Mohan Thakur is a Certified Paranormal Investigator and a Demonologist. He completed his Bachelor of Forensic Science from Dr. Harisingh Gour Vishwavidyalaya, Madhya Pradesh, India. He got his Paranormal Investigator Certification from Thomas Francis University, Florida, USA. He has done his Demonology from ParaLearning, UK. He is also a Member of the ParaNexus Anomalous Research Association, USA, and the International Alliance of Paranormal Investigators, UK

Printed by Libri Plureos GmbH in Hamburg, Germany